UP AND TO THE RIGHT

RIGHT

*Strategy and Tactics
of Analyst Influence*

Richard Stiennon

ISBN-13: 978-0-9854607-0-9

Cover design by Gil Lapastora

With thanks to Gene Kim for planting the inception

Table of Contents

About the author

Richard Stiennon was a VP Research at Gartner. He is a widely quoted and followed independent analyst that covers the IT security industry. He is the author of Surviving Cyberwar (Rowman&Littlefield, 2010). He was Chief Marketing Officer for Fortinet, and has held positions at Webroot Software and PricewaterhouseCoopers. He has presented in 26 countries on six continents. He writes the Cyber Domain blog for Forbes.com. He was named one of the "50 Most Powerful People in Networking" by Network World Magazine and was given Gartner's Thought Leadership Award in 2003. His experience on both sides of the analyst influence equation has led to the publication of this guide to influencing analysts.

CHAPTER ONE

A Story

In his *Essays in the Art of Writing,* Robert Louis Stevenson wrote "There is nothing so disenchanting than to be shown the springs and mechanisms of any art." This book exposes the springs and mechanisms of the art of analyst influence. The focus is on the much maligned, but supremely important, Gartner Magic Quadrant, a tool used by buyers to select technology products. Each vendor is represented by a dot on a simple graph. While the goal may be to move the dot UP and to the RIGHT, there are other rewards from following the strategies and tactics presented here. Influencing analysts is not just an exercise in targeting the perceptions that a few analysts at Gartner have of you, your company, and your product. It means managing all of the influencing factors that ultimately lead to that magic moment when the Gartner analyst compiles his or her spread sheets, examines the scatter shot result, and moves the dot for your product to its final position.

"Now wait a minute," you say. "The Gartner Magic Quadrants are just guides. They are not the ultimate arbiter of product selection. Everyone knows that the vendors in the Leaders Quadrant paid to get there. The positions of the various vendors in a quadrant are arbitrary, capricious, and determined by the subjective choice of the analyst. If you are misplaced it is because the analyst has a personal dislike for you or your product." These are some of the myths around the Gartner MQ. As a VP Research at Gartner until 2004 I was privy to how the process worked and I saw first hand the powerful impact your position in your industry's MQ could have on sales, growth, investor interest, and even ultimately the acquisition of a vendor based on their positioning in the upper right quadrant (the Leaders Quadrant.) I can attest to the fact that the "pay to play" myth is completely false. Often I did not even know the vendor was a Gartner client and I rarely knew the amounts they paid for Gartner research or to participate in Gartner events. I also had direct experience of vendors who did the right things to get my attention, win me over, and eventually influence their position in the Magic Quadrants I was responsible for.

Let me tell the story of the North American Enterprise Firewall Magic Quadrant during my stint at Gartner from 2000 to 2004. Keep in mind that in those earlier days Gartner had not refined its MQ methodology, it *was* more subjective than objective, which is something I will explore in depth in this book.

I was the third analyst to take on the Firewall MQ. I inherited an MQ that had mostly legacy vendors in it: Check Point, Cisco, Gauntlet, even Sidewinder and Raptor. It had been several years since there were any major moves of any of the dots. I came at the MQ from a fresh perspective and hoped to use the MQ to drive the vendors towards what I saw happening in the market.

Gartner's strength and market advantage in the research industry is its large client base. Today it has over 11,000 customers, mostly large enterprises, state and local governments, universities, and financial services firms. Gartner analysts derive their expertise from the continual interaction with the IT departments of these organizations. I remember thinking when I first joined Gartner that I may not have been an "expert" on the IT security industry when they hired me, but after six months of four to eight calls every single working day with CIOs and their teams, I *became* an expert. The questions posed in these "inquiries" from clients were often the same and could quickly be used to identify common concerns, popular trends in vendor selection, and an increasing level of interest in my particular area: network security.

At one point a vendor that had gone to market in the heady days of the Internet boom as a roll-up of security companies (Network Associates, Inc.) arranged to have a massive strategic engagement session with eight separate analysts. This was very unusual and very expensive--about $80K to get all the analysts to fly out to California to meet with the entire executive team led by Gene Hodges, president of NAI. It was a day-long review of each of the markets NAI played in. Years before NAI had acquired the Gauntlet firewall and it was the basis of their network security solution. There was just one problem: Over the previous year, out of several hundred inquiries about firewalls, just two were about Gauntlet. When it came time for me to present I flatly told the executive team it was time to "End of Life" the Gauntlet firewall. It did not have any market traction with the large enterprises that NAI was targeting and that comprised Gartner's customer base.

As I made my statement, backed up by my mentor, dialed in on the squawk box in the center of the long conference table, I looked around the room to judge the reaction. I saw heads nodding and eye contact being made. I knew that our advise was right on target and we were confirming a decision already contemplated by the executive team. What occurred next is a lesson in what happens when an analyst makes a bold call. The repercussions can impact the analyst's career and bring out the worst in a vendor.

When I drafted the next version of the Firewall Magic Quadrant I removed Gauntlet altogether. Keep in mind that Gauntlet had been carried over as a Leader and now I was erasing it. When I sent out the draft to all the vendors listed in the MQ I started to receive urgent calls from the the Gartner inquiry desk. The VP of marketing for NAI needed to talk to me. He was traveling in Europe but would make the time. When we connected, he was livid. "Not only are we the most visionary firewall vendor but we have the best ability to execute!" he shouted. These qualities, of course, are the two axes of the MQ. I told him that he should check with his executive team because perhaps I was privy to upper management sentiments that he was not. The next call I got was from one of the most senior analysts at Gartner. Ken McGee was old-school and had been with Gartner from the early days when everyone worked in the small building at the end of Top Gallant Road in Stamford, Connecticut, and Gideon Gartner was still at the helm. During my four day Gartner Boot Camp training Ken had come in to present on "Being a Curmudgeon." This was the first time I had ever taken a call from him. He wanted to say that the marketing guy from NAI was raising hell and wanted me fired. I explained the sequence of events and all he said was "check your facts and stick to your guns. We will support you all the way."

I published the MQ without Gauntlet and two

months later NAI announced the End of Life (EOL) of Gauntlet and passed the product off to Secure Computing, another vendor of firewalls. In a still unexplained twist of events NAI, now McAfee, acquired Secure Computing in 2008 before being acquired in turn by Intel in 2010.

Gartner analysts have to deal with irate marketing people all the time. It is a symptom of bad analysts relations (AR) and the frustration many vendors experience when dealing with Gartner. I will have more to say later about how *not* to react to unfavorable analyst coverage.

The Firewall MQ story does not end there. In 2003 a new network security technology was simultaneously developed by three new vendors. Intrusion prevention (IPS) was a technology developed to counter the threat of the day: worms and network attacks that could come in though open ports in a firewall. You might recall MS Blaster, SQL Slammer, Code Red and Nimda, all easily caught by IPS. It seemed to me that eventually firewalls would have to incorporate IPS if they were going to remain effective as the primary gateway security solution. I used the Firewall MQ to communicate this to the Gartner client base. I moved all of the Leaders at the time (including Cisco, Check Point, and Netscreen) to the Challengers Quadrant and informed the vendors that no one would be put in the Leaders Quadrant until they incorporated IPS capability into their firewalls. Netscreen was the first to make a move. They acquired an IPS vendor, One Secure, and I moved them to the Leaders Quadrant all on their own. Netscreen went public and was quickly snapped up by Juniper Networks for a cool $4.1 billion. I am not claiming credit for causing that tremendous success story, but it is a great example of how an analyst can be on top of a market, see what is coming on the horizon, and leverage the MQ to inform and influence.

This book is not about the IT security market even though this is one of the more vibrant spaces. Analyst coverage at Gartner grew from two of us in the Networking Group to what is today a separate security research group with close to forty analysts. This book is meant to provide actionable tactics and strategy for any vendor in the Information Technology industry. My perspective is derived first from my experience at PricewaterhouseCoopers as a consumer of analyst research, followed by four years on the inside as I watched Gartner go through the tumultuous dot-com bust and evolve into the industry dominant force it is today, then to my experience at two vendors, Webroot Software, and Fortinet, Inc. where I struggled with adverse analyst perceptions, and finally from my experience building an independent analyst practice over the last seven years and helping many clients create their analyst influence strategies.

As an independent analyst I am only a small cog in the analyst machine. Vendors make up 90% of my clients and all of them struggle with the same frustration with the Gartner Magic Quadrant process: it's expensive, confusing, and takes a tremendous amount of effort, often with no positive results.

You know that frustration. You know you have great technology--certainly better than your competitors'. You know that you are growing rapidly. You know that Gartner's own clients choose your product over your competitors' all the time. Yet the analyst just does not seem to get it. You are pigeon-holed in the wrong category. Your innovations are not recognized. Your channel strategy does not match your analyst's ideal. The analyst does not see the tidal wave coming that you are riding. Your interactions are confrontational and the sales team is clamoring for you to do something to make their jobs easier.

This book will give you the guidance you need to overcome these frustrations. It is a no-hype guide to things that work. It is a framework that takes into account the vastly different influence equation since the rise of bloggers and social media. I draw on my own experience and that of AR pros I have worked with, as well as other industry analysts, to identify the tactics and strategies you need to follow if you are going to move the dot UP and to the RIGHT.

If you are an executive at a technology company or an investor in those companies, a marketing professional, or an analyst relations person, you will find this book to be a distillation of the advice I provide to my clients that works to get your products and company recognized for its ability to execute and its completeness of vision. I have given internal seminars to train marketing teams in these techniques. I have helped early stage companies get positioned on their respective Magic Quadrant, sometimes with just the simplest advice. I have practical insight into what works and what does not. Read on!

CHAPTER TWO

The Magic of Magic Quadrants

There is magic in the Gartner Magic Quadrant. Despite the heaps of scorn expressed by vendors that don't make it into the Leaders Quadrant there is no denying the positive benefits that derive from reaching the position farthest UP and to the RIGHT. In this chapter I explain how an analyst creates a Magic Quadrant and what you should do to facilitate that process.

But first a few words about that magic. Here are some of the benefits that derive from favorable placement in the Magic Quadrant for your product category.

Increased deal participation

While many CIOs will claim that they don't rely on Gartner MQs, the reality is that being one of the three or four vendors in the Leaders Quadrant almost guarantees your inclusion in a product selection process. And, after all, what more do you need to win deals? Your product *is* the best, right? At the very least, most decision makers at large enterprises will want to know why you are not included in the bake-off and the supporting staff will have to justify the decision to leave you out. The most frequent complaint you will hear from your sales team, if you are not in the Leaders Quadrant, is that they don't get asked to the party because of the low ranking in the MQ. Increased deal participation more than justifies any effort or expense you make on behalf of moving the dot UP and to the RIGHT.

Increased valuation

It is hard to make the case for increased company valuation based on position in the Magic Quadrant. The hard evidence is not there. But anecdotal evidence abounds. I told the story of Netscreen and its $4.1 billion valuation in the Introduction, and based on investor interest in Magic Quadrants, you know that they pay attention to placement. Every company that has acquired a Leader does not fail to mention that in the press release or in their Power Point presentations to customers and investors. S-1 filings for IPOs invariably mention Magic Quadrant placement if it is anything but Niche.

Press relations

Every time a new MQ comes out you have an opportunity to issue a self congratulatory press release. This, incidentally, serves to promulgate the power of the Magic Quadrant for Gartner. Being in the

Magic Quadrant is often table stakes for being included in the trade press reviews and other analyst firms pay attention to the vendors in the MQ.

M&A activity

Since the Gartner Magic Quadrants are often the best market summary for a particular space it is inevitable that those involved in mergers and acquisitions use the MQ as a baseline in their due diligence. All the other benefits listed here aside, there is a real cost associated with attaining Leader status and an acquirer recognizes that buying the Leader means they will expend less on fighting the MQ battle post acquisition.

What is the Magic Quadrant?

For every product or service category that warrants it, Gartner analysts create and publish a research note called the Gartner Magic Quadrant. This document describes the current state of the market. Drivers for the market are highlighted as well as macro factors such as the economy and major shifts in demand or technology. Key criteria are included and a synopsis describing each vendor is provided. The document is built around a simple graphic: a square broken into four quadrants. The two axes are Ability to Execute (vertical) and Completeness of Vision (horizontal.)

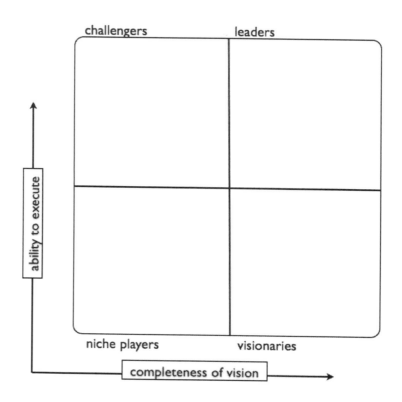

Ability to Execute

This is the business side of the measurement. Ability to execute is a measure of a vendor's ability to scale to meet demand while keeping up the pace of innovation. This is where executive management team experience and track record is considered. A publicly traded company, which has readier access to capital and transparency in its performance, gets a heavier weighting than a private company. Other crucial factors:

Partnerships

Does the vendor have an eco-system of partners whose products integrate with theirs? Have they engaged major channels such as IBM Global Services or one of the large consulting firms such as Deloitte or PwC to help sell their products?

Reference customers

Remember that the analyst probably does not have hands-on experience with your product. He does, however, know the buyers at the largest companies in the world and gives a lot of weight to their purchasing decisions.

Channel strategy

Direct? Multi-tier distribution? Hybrid? It is typical for a young company to be 100% direct. They have not built the momentum to attract resellers and through them, distributors. Established vendors who have crossed Geoffrey Moore's Chasm are typically 100% channel. Analysts tend to have a prejudice in favor of that 100% channel strategy since it is an indicator of company maturity.

Geographic placement

Let's face it, companies in certain locations tend to

become market leaders. They have to be close to their customers or close to a supply of employees. To an analyst, a technology company in Florida is likely to be viewed as motivated by easy living and lifestyle choices instead of access to resources and clients. It is no mystery why Marc Andreesen packed up his bags and moved to Silicon Valley to found Netscape.

Geographic dispersion

An analyst will look at the global reach of a vendor to determine where it is on its growth curve. Are EU offices limited to one in Brussels or the UK? Or, for a European vendor, is there only one US office in New Jersey? Typically Leaders have multiple sales offices, and often development, support, and manufacturing, in North America, EMEA, and Asia. As LATAM develops, it too will be included as an indicator of ability to execute.

Revenue distribution

An analyst will look for the percentage breakdown of revenue from each major region. The expectation is that more than 50% of sales will come from the US market, reflecting the giant size of the IT market in the United States. If a US vendor derives 70% or more from the US market that is an indication of early growth phase and the need for additional investment in global expansion. The same goes for EMEA or AsiaPAC vendors. If the source of revenue indicates a local aspect, ability to execute may be impaired.

Research and development expenditures

Analysts are interested in the overall size of an R&D department compared to the rest of the organization. Vendors will often attempt to inflate this metric by lumping sales engineers in with development. A company that is under-investing in engineering is one that may not stay competitive or is milking its installed base for profitability to please Wall Street.

Support

One measure that is often derived from an analyst's conversations with your customers is the quality of your support. In the 90s Cisco was known for its manic attention to customer support. Customers would resist switching vendors just based on the fear of losing their relationship with the Cisco engineers they trusted. An analyst can be deeply swayed by reports that your customer support is plagued with long waits on the phone, failure to return calls, and long delays getting replacement products (RMA). Conversely, an analyst will be favorably impressed by reports of outstanding support.

Marketing strategy

Analysts of all people understand the importance of a well thought out marketing strategy and execution on that strategy. Sure, there are the Googles of the world that create products customers need and don't bother with marketing. But there are also the Apples that focus the entire company on product design, quality, and marketing. You don't want the answer to "How do you market your product?" to be "Word of mouth."

Completeness of vision

The horizontal axis of the Magic Quadrant is a measure of completeness of vision. There is no getting around the fact that this means the analyst's vision, not yours. You have to understand what the analyst considers when compiling these measures.

Comprehensive features

Most technology vendors start out with a single product that addresses a single problem. Over time as customer requirements are incorporated the number of features grow to the point where the product is a complete solution that contributes to customer productivity. The first word processors did little more than what a typewriter could do with the added ability to quickly revise documents. As the market evolved, and Microsoft Word eventually won, word processing software turned into massive productivity suites for the office with spreadsheets, presentation software, macros, and integration with automated systems. Completeness of vision in the early days might have included support for multiple non-standard fonts.

Today it would include the integration with cloud storage, encryption, and publishing capabilities to Kindle and Print on Demand sources.

Innovation

Analysts look for evidence that a vendor is pushing the envelope and defining the required features in their product category. Are the other vendors behind you? Are they scrambling to introduce features that you invented? Are they losing deals to you based on your innovations?

Product narrative

It is critical that a vendor be able to articulate why they are in business and why their products address the needs of the market. Large vendors such as IBM, CA, EMC, even Cisco, are most challenged by this requirement. How can they articulate a strategy around telepresence in Cisco's case, when there is no hiding the fact that they are a routing and switching company? How could Coke convince an analyst that they are in the quality-of-life-enhancement business when in fact they are marketers and licensors of sweetened carbonated beverages? This is why the largest vendors invariably end up in the upper left Quadrant: Challengers. They have massive presence and thus ability to execute but their vision is clouded by their other interests.

Customer references

On this axis the key customer reference is the one who says "we chose this vendor because they solved a problem no one else could." If enough Gartner clients report a similar need for a feature or capability that only you have addressed, that will be the most influential aspect on your Completeness of Vision.

The Four Quadrants

The existence of two axes that bisect a square creates four quadrants. The MQ research note provides a synopsis of each vendor organized into these four categories:

Niche

The Niche Quadrant is where most new vendors to the MQ start out -either their revenue is too low or their product only serves a limited segment of the Gartner client base. Becoming a new participant in an MQ is usually a great thing for a vendor. It can serve to jump start their sales. They are on the map. However, moving from any of the other quadrants to the Niche Quadrant is considered a disaster. It means that the vendor has failed to innovate if their last position was Visionary or they are rapidly losing relevance in the market if they had been a Challenger. The best path for a Niche vendor is to move to the right into Visionary and then cross the line up and into the Leaders Quadrant.

Visionary

Vendors in the Visionary Quadrant have industry leading products but do not have the revenue, global reach, partnerships, and channel organization to be Leaders. Vendors should strive to be the farthest to the right (the most visionary). Often Challengers will acquire Visionary vendors in the hopes that with their ability to execute they will quickly boost the company into the Leaders Quadrant, an exercise in vector addition that does not always work.

Challenger

It is not a bad thing to be a Challenger. It usually implies that the vendor has a large installed base, tremendous resources, and has been around for a while. In many markets the Challengers represent the ones to beat in most enterprise sales situations. These are the entrenched vendors. They are bad at coming up with new products and features which is a natural outcome of having many customers and legacy products to support. If there is a fast moving trend in their space they will acquire a young company for their technology and people. Very few Challengers are also good integrators of acquisitions. Too often the acquisition appears to disappear from the market.

Leaders

This is the goal--getting to the Leaders Quadrant. It means you have exceptional products and the ability to grow with demand while continuing to invest in new features and respond rapidly to changing customer needs. But the game is not over. The Leaders Quadrant defines your primary competitors. You want to be Up and to the RIGHT of all of them.

Of course all of these factors are considered in a different light depending on the overall maturity of a market. An MQ for Enterprise Resource Planning (ERP) or Business Process Intelligence (BPI) is going to have different requirements for Ability to Execute and Completeness of Vision than an MQ for bio-informatics, or cloud services.

Wow! These are stringent requirements. How can you even hope to influence an analyst when they use such objective criteria? Well, the assumption is that you have all of these qualities, that your products are great, your customers love you, and you are on a roll. Otherwise, how could you hope to be a market leader? You can fool the analysts for a short time, especially in a newly emerging product category, but in the long run the analyst will figure it out. The purpose of analyst influence is to make sure they know of your qualities. And analysts are human. They derive clues that shape their judgement from many sources. If someone they respect, the CIO at a major bank, raves about your product or company, they are going to give you the benefit of increased attention. If they see your company on the front page of the Wall Street Journal for doing something game-changing they are going to take that into account. If they see positive comments posted to Twitter and forums about your company they will be swayed to view you in a positive light. If they realize that your customer support issues come from a brief glitch in your software updates they will take that into account. So read on because influence, in all its various forms, works.

The Creation of a Magic Quadrant

Here is how Magic Quadrants are created. This is based on my four years as the primary author of two Magic Quadrants and secondary author on several more. It is also derived from my knowledge of changes to the process since I left. Thanks to frequent challenges to their process and objectivity from disgruntled vendors, Gartner has put a lot of work into improving their process. I also work with many vendors on their responses to the surveys Gartner sends out for Magic Quadrants so I have seen this evolution first hand.

Each Magic Quadrant has at least one primary author and possibly several secondary authors depending on the size and importance of a product category. The responsibility for creating an MQ is the most onerous task a Gartner Analyst has. (Creating 18 slide PowerPoint presentations for Summits and Symposia is the next most onerous task.) Analysts dread the process. They like to be thinking about and researching the next big thing, not re-hashing ground they covered over and over.

In most cases the MQ for a particular category already exists. The analyst either was present at the inception or inherited the MQ from another analyst who has moved up, moved on to other areas of coverage, or left Gartner altogether. There is surprisingly little support structure at Gartner--no research assistants, secretaries, fact checkers, or Business Intelligence tools to help them. There is a huge staff of editors but they are often a hindrance, not a help. Gartner editors make sure that Research Notes are in the "Gartner voice", thus eliminating the opportunity for an analyst to imbue his or her research with his own voice and flavor of discourse. Gartner analysts are individual contributors and remarkably free from the day to day hassles you would expect from a highly paid professional, often with the title of Vice President. They have no direct-reports, thus no employee evaluations to fill out, and few meetings, except by conference call to discuss research agendas and coordinate Summit activities. They work from home and are often on the road. Other than producing Research Notes and presentations the vast majority of their time is taken up with briefings and inquiries--predominantly over the phone.

The publication of MQs used to be scheduled to coincide with the Gartner IT Symposium at Disney World every fall, but today that is not adhered to as strictly. Symposium is a massive event with close to 10,000 attendees from the Gartner client base and over 150 vendors with booths in the Exposition area. It is a week long extravaganza of keynotes from the CEOs of top technology firms. Bill Gates, Steve Balmer, Steve Jobs, and Larry Ellison have all been on the main stage at Symposium. Each analyst has several sessions to present as well as grueling hours in rat-maze booths doing one-on-one meetings with vendors and end-users. Their presentations are supposed to include updated Magic Quadrants for their sectors. Often the official schedule for MQs is for a new one to appear every six months. Because of the tremendous work load, this often gets collapsed into one every twelve months, which is actually a blessing for the vendors. Responding to the MQ surveys is an arduous task too.

First the analyst must decide who makes the cut for the next version of the MQ. They look at all the vendors who have been acquired or, thanks to their inside knowledge, are about to be acquired. They determine what the inclusion criteria will be, often a gross revenue measure but sometimes a new requirement based on changes to the market. Throughout the year they would have been making notes about new vendors to include, usually as Niche vendors, based on the 100-200 vendor briefings they have participated in.

The analyst then refines the spreadsheet containing the 20-150 questions that are going to be used to generated the positions in the Magic Quadrant. In addition to the actual questions, they come up with the secret weightings that are applied to each answer from each vendor. The questionnaires are usually broken down into business questions and product capability questions that line up with the Ability to Execute and Completeness of Vision axes.

The analyst must then send the questionnaire to the contact person on record at each vendor. This is the part they dread. It is the official kick-off of the vendor response cycle. Savvy vendors use this phase to schedule briefings and inquiries (if they are clients) to get clarification on what the analyst is thinking. It could mean fifteen or more scheduled calls for the analyst, all to discuss the upcoming MQ.

When the vendors respond by the required time, with the usual pleas for extensions, the responses are reviewed and combined into one spreadsheet. A score, or rating, is given to each answer, and each question has a weight associated with it: low-standard-high. At the press of a button the ratings and weights are applied and the Magic Quadrant is created! Well, that is how it would work in an ideal world. In reality, each vendor responds with different units, different time scales (oh, you meant *calendar* quarters!), and often just confusing entries. The analyst has to determine if the reported revenue is bookings, sales, or even if the vendor pulled some slight-of-hand reporting list price sales instead of discounted sales, or whether they bundle services and consulting into product revenue.

It's a nightmare.

Once all the data is normalized and perhaps adjusted to reflect reality, an MQ is generated. Now comes the subjective part. The spreadsheet tool may cluster all the respective dots from all the vendors around the crosshairs--all the vendors are almost the same in ability to execute and completeness of vision. No problem, the scale is adjusted to spread them out. Then the analyst does a reality check. Does that vendor with the slick product but only 25 employees really belong in the Leaders Quadrant? Is IBM really a niche vendor in the space? How did the company that was first to market fall below the line into Visionary? How has the picture changed from the year before-- can the major moves be explained?

After all the adjustments, and a review by the other analysts to get buy-in, the draft MQ is sent to all the participating vendors along with the brief synopsis of their company and product that will be in the main body of the research note. Then the fun begins. Every vendor who is not happy with their placement makes urgent requests for briefings to clarify their position or argue why they are so much better than the vendors ranked above them. Even the vendors placed in the Leaders Quadrant will not be happy unless they are the farthest UP and to the RIGHT. Every word of the synopsis will be scrutinized by the vendor and they will lobby for minor changes that portray them in a better light. Vendors have been known to *count* the number of words devoted to them and attempt to bring that number inline with their competitors' count.

Finally the analyst will complete the vendor response phase and send the MQ off to editing where it is scrubbed for language compliance and formatted for publication. It is out of the analyst's hands. She breathes a sigh of relief and moves on to the other MQ for which she is responsible.

Now that we have examined the Magic Quadrant, and the process to create it, let's turn to the topic of how you can influence this process to your advantage.

CHAPTER THREE
Influence

Influence is not just analyst relations. Analyst relations is just the mechanics of interacting with analysts. There are hundreds of analyst firms, it just happens that Gartner is by far the biggest and the Magic Quadrant is the single-most powerful ranking of vendors. You need an active AR effort to oversee the entire process of moving the dot UP and to the RIGHT, but becoming the real leader in any space is a whole-of-organization endeavor. The dominant players in any market should be in the Leaders Quadrant. The up-and-coming players can leverage a favorable position in the MQ to become dominant forces in their industry.

Market dominance is obviously the goal of most commercial enterprises. With market dominance comes lower sales costs, potentially lower marketing costs, and higher margins--all things that executive management strives for and stockholders hope to see.

The key point is that analyst influence is an integral part of the organization's goals. Because it has so many components, executing an analyst influence strategy means having a complete go-to-market strategy that covers all the bases.

When Gideon Gartner invented the concept of industry analysts the IT world was a different place. For all practical purposes there were two technology companies: IBM and Amdahl. If there had been Magic Quadrants in those days, IBM would have been the Leader and Amdahl the scrappy Visionary. Univac, Honeywell, and Fujistu were biting at their heels and would have been scattered throughout the MQ. The customers of these mainframe vendors were predominantly governments and big banks. IBM was the dominant player and charged humongous fees for installing and maintaining rooms full of giant computing machines and peripherals. Amdahl was practically a clone of IBM and offered a lower cost product at arguably better value. How was a bank to decide which one to go with? They needed guidance. Gideon Gartner to the rescue. He created a company which in his words "provided Buy-Hold-Sell advice" to technology consumers. His innovation was modeled off Wall Street analysis of securities.

Gartner customers would subscribe to printed research reports produced by a handful of analysts and sent out every month. They were printed on three hole punch paper so their clients could insert them in special ring binders.

Today Gartner is an industry powerhouse with 12,000 clients and 800 analysts. Total revenue is $1.5

billion. They have acquired Meta and Burton Group. However, available information to help make purchase decisions of technology products has grown much faster than Gartner. Let's look at some of these sources. All of them are going to be part of our analyst influence strategy.

Google

While I was at Gartner there was a mini-backlash from industry against analyst firms. In the early part of the century (I like saying that) the refrain was "who needs Gartner when I can find any information I need using Google?" True, Google is the primary research tool for anyone investigating technology. A quick search on a product category will reveal most of the vendors in the organic results--at least those that have done a good job on their SEO (Search Engine Optimization), and the ads in the right hand column of search results will often reveal many more. Now try to discover the size of a particular market. Pose the question "how big is the online backup industry?" and see what you get. Invariably, you will be led to a market report by a research firm. The abstract of the report will not answer your question and you will be asked to purchase the complete report. If you are researching a particular product you can find forum entries where end-users discuss the issues they are having. You can even find a Wikipedia entry where you will get a dry summary of the products, services, and history of the vendor. Google does not even come close to replacing the value of knowledgeable experts with whom you can get on the phone and have the input of someone who probably has hands on experience with the product and has talked to hundreds of end-user clients of the product. That said, Google has its uses and analysts leverage them. They do periodic Google searches on the companies they track, and they set up Google alerts on vendors so they get early notice of news-making events, often before your PR firm has issued a press release. Google blog alerts will let an analyst know when someone is writing about your products or company. Analysts are information junkies. They absorb everything in their field to stay current and to get ideas of new trends. So it is critical that you monitor your own Google alerts, if only to be aware of what the analysts are seeing. You can also use SEO techniques to ensure that you appear in the top search results on terms the analyst is likely to use. Has your analyst coined a term to categorize your industry? Strive to be the top result for that term. Do you purchase keywords based on your competitor's product names? That may seem underhanded and it *is* a little dirty, but have you checked to make sure your competitors aren't already doing that? The most likely term an analyst will search on? His own name! Think about how you can leverage that human frailty. We will come back to it in the chapter on guerrilla analyst influence.

Wikipedia

Yes, analysts use Wikipedia, even if only for fact checking. Wikipedia is a great source of company history and sometimes it is easier and faster to check on the identity of executive management through Wikipedia than through a company's web site. And you do not have direct control over what appears in your own Wikipedia entry. I will cover some work-arounds for that problem in a later chapter.

Bloggers

The vast blogging community is becoming a powerful influence. Every traditional media organization has been challenged by the rise of bloggers. Individual bloggers can sway public opinion or build on the general consensus, and negative blogging is much more predominant that positive. Just as newspapers gravitate towards bad news, it seems like human nature to accentuate the negative. There are multiple, sometimes hundreds, of blogs devoted to every speciality in the IT industry, and analysts read them. Identify key bloggers in your space. Follow them on Twitter. Read and comment on their posts. Support them with access to your key people. Give them scoops on new products, personnel, or major news items. Ignore them at your peril.

Online tech press

Everyone in technology reads the new breed of online tech press--ArsTechnica, TechCrunch, Wired,

Mashable, etc. especially analysts. Yes, they lean towards cool gadgets and the latest mobile phone or iPad or consumer cloud service, but you have cool products don't you? Make sure that your PR efforts focus on these media, even overweigh the amount of effort devoted to getting positive coverage from them.

Trade press

The trade press has been hit hard by new media. They have struggled to come up with new models. United Business Media is a great example of a publisher that is finding their way in this new world. They spin up new sites with communities, interactive forums and events at an alarming rate (alarming to the poor PR team tasked with keeping up). InternetEvolution, ITServices, Light Reading, and Dark Reading are just a few of the sites they have created, usually with vendor sponsorships of the content. Consider sponsoring such a site and at the very least keep your eye on what they are covering.

Newspapers

Although the demise of newspapers has been predicted by pundits I believe they too will survive. They are still the curators of news as it is happening and the record of events that will soon be part of history. Most newspapers have managed the transition to a hybrid model of online for breaking news and print for something to read over breakfast. If you read a newspaper from cover to cover (as I do, especially when traveling) you feel that you are caught up on the last 24 hours. Analysts read newspapers, especially Gartner analysts. They are old school. You could even say that as a group they are late adaptors. Do not neglect the traditional PR activities that get you seen in newspapers. One other thing to consider that I also cover in guerrilla techniques is that Gartner tracks and reports on analyst quotes in mainstream media: CNN, USA Today, Le Monde, the *Financial Times*, the *Wall Street Journal*, even the *San Jose Mercury News* (Gartner's second largest office is located in San Jose, California). That tracking is for internal use only, of course.

Don't forget the de-facto analyst/journalists. The best example is Walt Mossberg (WSJ), possibly the highest paid tech influencer in the world. If your product has a consumer or small business application, get to know Mossberg and work to get him to be aware of you. A mention in his column is golden and will most likely be seen by the analysts you are trying to influence. He may not cover your space but I bet you could hold a private dinner and invite analysts to attend. They will come if the featured guest is Walt Mossberg.

Twitter

Twitter is a powerful tool for influence. Most analysts have Twitter accounts; many are extremely active. See the social media chapter for more on leveraging Twitter for analyst influence.

LinkedIn

LinkedIn is becoming a valuable tool for industry analysts. Not only does it connect them directly with your executive team but your sales force and channel is busy connecting to industry analysts. While you are still formulating your analyst influence strategy members of your team may be ahead of you! You have to reign them in and provide strict guidelines to control those connections. Keep in mind that LinkedIn is providing data on employee turnover, where your departing employees go, and where your new hires come from. A savvy analyst will be tracking that.

Facebook

I am not sold on Facebook's efficacy for business, but go ahead and create and maintain a Facebook page. Invite industry analysts to "like" it. That alone is a hard thing to do. Analysts don't indicate that they like a vendor lightly. They are repelled by the idea that all of their "friends" will see that status update on their wall; it feels like an endorsement. If you can get them past that revulsion, you have a great vehicle for hammering them with news and event information. Pictures of the huge crowds having a good time at your annual convention or sales meeting seem popular.

Other analyst firms

Many advisors treat Forrester and IDC like stepping stones to influencing Gartner. From my experience this does not work at all. Gartner analysts are oblivious to what other analyst firms say. They just don't care. They are the major leagues and the other firms the minor leagues. If anything, Gartner analysts are prone to push back on the findings of other firms. If IDC coins a new term for a product category Gartner will coin their own and define it differently. The other firms have analysts that are influencers in their own right and therefore deserve courting. They may not influence Gartner analysts but they influence Gartner clients.

Books

There is no denying that books can be extremely influential. A *New York Times* Bestseller from Malcolm Gladwell, or Clayton M. Christensen's books on the Innovator's Dilemma will quickly make the rounds of the analyst community. Analysts still read books. Think about how you can leverage that. Mainstream publishers usually don't get around to putting out books until there is a large community of users of a product. Work with a publisher to get a book written on your product area using examples/ screenshots from your product. Encourage your CTO to write the book and take it to Syngress or any of the other tech publishers. Send autographed copies to all the people on your targeted list of influencers. Even if they don't read it they will let it sit on their desk for months. That is much better than a coffee mug or mouse pad for reminding the influencer of your thought leadership.

YouTube

I am not a big fan of strategies to create a viral video for products or vendors. I have seen horrible attempts at viral videos by vendors. The only product videos I have seen go viral are ones that are made by end-users and they are extremely negative. Do create a body of videos that demonstrate the strength of your products. Interviews with your CEO or CTO are great ways for customers, journalists, and yes, analysts, to get to know your company through its primary evangelists. Create product demo videos, too. You may not always be able to schedule a one-on-one demo with an analyst but if they have a link to a professionally produced video they may watch it when they are researching the MQ. Imagine the power of that! (Full disclosure: IT-Harvest has produced over 50 professional video interviews with vendor executives over the last two years. We have realized that many vendors have yet to tap into this method of getting the word out on what they do and who they are. There are also services such as Demos On Demand that turn slick video demos into lead generation and sales tools integrated with Salesforce.com.)

The vendors I have seen with the best video

strategy create a YouTube Channel and populate it with dozens of videos, many of them training videos on their products presented by their key experts and executives.

If you are feeling audacious (and ready to spend $100K+) you could hire John Cleese or some other actor/comedian popular with the tech crowd to act in one of your videos. That would get you some positive attention. Maybe it *is* possible to create a good viral video.

Independent analysts

I can't leave myself out of the story. I am an independent analyst. Barbara French curates the analyst directory at

analystdirectory.barbarafrench.net

She lists over 650 independent analyst firms and there are probably about two thousand analysts worldwide who are making a living at it on their own. Working with such analysts is a different matter than working with the big analyst firms. Often they are powerful voices in their industry with the same name recognition as their counterparts at Gartner. They may even be former Gartner, Forester, or IDC analysts. They are usually more prolific than big firm analysts and have active and popular blogs. Many of them have long standing relationships with the press and are quoted often in the main stream media. Think of Rob Enderle as the prime example of such an analyst. Work with independent analysts. Hire them to write white papers, host your webinars and breakfast seminars, and provide strategy guidance. If they are former Gartner analysts they can provide insights into the process and maybe even into the personalities and life stories of the analysts you are targeting. OK, enough with the plug. On to bigger and better things: The Influence Pyramid.

CHAPTER FOUR

The Influence Pyramid

Think of your influence strategy as a giant pyramid. At every level of the pyramid you exert influence and at every level you reap rewards. As you work your way up the pyramid you focus more and more on the end goal: moving your placement in the Magic Quadrant UP and to the RIGHT.

The bottom of the pyramid is your addressable market as represented by the people who make purchasing decisions in your space. One important factor to keep in mind is that influence flows both ways, but the influence that flows from the bottom up is cumulative while the influence that flows down is targeted. As you succeed in influencing one level the rewards flow downhill and result in increased sales or shorter sales cycles. All good.

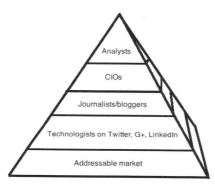

THE INFLUENCE PYRAMID

Every customer can be an influence on the rest of the addressable market, resulting in an immediate impact on your sales. Over time, as you get more customers you get more of the base of the pyramid supporting your position in the world. It is also very hard to shake your position at the top (the cumulative influence you have on the Gartner analyst) if you have a dominant position in the base.

Customers also influence the next level: technology users who are on social media, many of whom are also customers. However, it is your job to maintain a constant effort to generate positive tweets or at least recognition from these part-time influencers. Part-time because most of the time they are talking about Justin Bieber and the Super Bowl, but they are connected to the next tier and many important influencers in your space--sometimes even the analysts.

The third tier is comprised of the bloggers and journalists who cover your space. They pick up on the general sentiment of the tiers below them which then influences what they say and how they cover your company and products. That, in turn, influences the next tier.

The CIOs. Why break the CIOs out from the bottom tier of customer decision makers? It is because of the influence they exert upwards on the analyst community. On the way up the pyramid you want to get to the C-level decision makers. By building a strong sentiment that favors your company, gets it noticed, gets you invited to demo and sell your products, you are creating a self-financing strategy. Any effort to market to the lowest tier, engage the social media tier, work with the bloggers and journalists, will pay off as the CIOs include you in their IT strategies. And from the CIOs comes your primary influence on Gartner.

Before talking about how CIOs influence Gartner, let's return to your influence strategy at the lower tiers. Every action you take to influence any tier serves the ultimate goal of influencing analysts. The results are simply more diffuse so it takes a lot of touch points. Despite my somewhat forced metaphor of a pyramid, the analyst community is connected to all these tiers. They engage with decision makers at all levels. They talk to the channel to discover what products are selling and what the success rate is of installations of these products. If there is a positive vibe associated with your company from the bottom to the top analysts will pick up on it.

Now let's talk about those CIOs. Gartner analysts talk every day to CIOs in their client base. Think of the Gartner client base as the Global 10,000 (that is certainly what they want the market to do.) A Gartner analyst may talk to as many as twenty CIOs in a week through the inquiry process and one-on-one meetings at conferences and sales calls. By the topics of these conversations they draw conclusions about what is hot--which categories are seeing a surge in interest, which vendors are making it to the bake-offs. If a Gartner analyst gets three calls a week where your company comes up they will conclude that you are gaining tremendous traction. *There is no better way to influence a Gartner analyst than through the Gartner client base.*

A word about the Gartner client base. Gartner classifies buyers into categories and is the first to admit that 80% of their clients are late adaptors. Think of Geoffrey Moore's *Crossing the Chasm* theory again. It is only after you begin to be picked up by late adaptors that your company starts to dominate an industry. Think of the qualities of a late adaptor: large, risk averse, tons of legacy products still in their IT shops. They have extensive IT staffs, long evaluation cycles, and often refuse to be reference clients. In short they are hard to sell to. CIOs at late adaptors are the type of people who do not make a move without checking with Gartner. If you *are* selling to them, the Gartner analyst will pick up on that and will finally be ready to move you UP and to the RIGHT in the Magic Quadrant.

That is just the first half of the cycle. Getting positive positioning in the MQ immediately cascades down to all the lower tiers in the pyramid. You start to gain a bigger chunk of the market (the base). You get more attention in social media and from bloggers and journalists and that leads to more assurance to the CIOs at the late adaptors that it is time to look at your products. That in turn feeds the analysts with more data, and affirmation that they were right, which generates future positive change to your position in the Magic Quadrant.

That is how it works. Now, how can you deploy your resources to influence each tier of the pyramid with a tighter and tighter focus as you reach the top?

CHAPTER FIVE
The MQ Strategy

You cannot have a strategy if you have not set a goal.

The very first step in creating an MQ strategy is to decide which Magic Quadrants you are going to target. If you are already positioned in a Magic Quadrant this step is easy, unless you want to attempt a move to a different MQ or--the hardest task of all-- see a new Magic Quadrant created.

Let's get that one out of the way now. While it is possible to wield your influence to get a new MQ or to re-define an existing one, there are almost insurmountable barriers to doing so. The biggest barrier is the analyst. I already described how much work goes into creating and maintaining a Magic Quadrant. Many analysts are brought to tears at the very thought of adding to their burden. They are well-versed on pushing back at vendors who always (in the analyst's mind) want to create a category with themselves as the sole provider. This is a non-starter. Only after an analyst sees a market develop (a market for late adaptors don't forget) will they begin to contemplate a new MQ. Your best option is to target a junior analyst who may not have an MQ to his or her name yet. They need to make their mark on the world and are more willing to cover an emerging space.

The first indication that a new MQ is in the works is the Market Scope Research Note. This has all the appearance of a Magic Quadrant without the Quadrant graphic and there is no commitment to maintaining it year after year. Set your expectations at about two years to see a Market Scope created. If the space is developing rapidly, that could turn into an MQ within an additional six months, but more likely a year.

Now, on to the more traditional scope of an existing MQ. If you are not on a Magic Quadrant you must pick one, which is usually an easy task: it is the one that contains all of your competitors.

If possible, see if you can obtain the most recent questionnaire that was used to gather the inputs for your Magic Quadrant. Of course this is a proprietary document that may be hard to get. I suggest asking the analyst. It can't hurt to ask and, at the very least, the analyst may share the key criteria with you over the phone.

It is easier to obtain historical copies of the Magic Quadrants going back several years. The Leaders often make them available on their web sites. They had to pay Gartner for the right to do that. Get them and study them. The document explains the key criteria. From reviewing the historical Research Notes you will be able to see how the industry, and Gartner's perception of it, has changed over the years.

The next step is to take an honest look at your company and your products. If you were creating this MQ where would you position your company? And don't answer "to the right and above every vendor on it."

Analysts can miss a vendor, especially if they are in a non-English speaking region like China, but it is extremely unlikely that they miss a vendor that belongs in the Leaders Quadrant. Analysts can certainly be blind to your presence or impact on your space, especially if you do not yet sell to the Global 10,000; but that is what we are addressing with this strategy.

Make an *honest* assessment. Create a chart of the key criteria that the analyst has explicitly defined in the MQ. Add your estimates of the revenue, number of employees, number of deployments, partnerships, etc. for each of the vendors in the MQ. Line your own company up with that competitive analysis (something you probably should have done already) and see where you fall.

Look at your closest competitor in the MQ. If you can make the case that you have more revenue, customer wins, and global presence, as well as a better product, you can target getting to at least the level of that competitor. If you execute on your strategy you should be able to get there in a couple of cycles of the Magic Quadrant.

That is the strategy for getting your first placement on the Magic Quadrant. Longer term you should have a strategy for getting to the optimum position in the MQ. Most vendors and their investors or stock holders would say the goal is to be the furthest UP and to the RIGHT in the Leaders Quadrant. But that is not always the case. If you have made the decision to only address a niche market, such as education, government, or Southeast Michigan, your target may be the furthest UP and to the RIGHT in the Niche Quadrant.

You know your company's growth targets. You have estimates of revenue and other key factors for the other participants in the MQ. Line them up. You should be able to plot positions in the MQ that match your growth trajectory. Don't forget that the Magic Quadrant is really a moving snapshot of a space. Most IT sectors are growing at a good pace. If the MQs had fixed criteria, over time every healthy vendor would move UP and to the RIGHT until they were all bunched together in the upper right-hand corner. But the MQ is a snapshot of the relative position of all the vendors in *relation to each other*. Do not assume that your competitors are going to stand still. Competition is a race after all. Your strategy should be to give yourself every advantage in that race by positioning yourself ahead of where your completely objective position should be. You do that by following the guidance in this book.

Now you have a goal. Put a blown up printout of

the MQ on your wall and push a pin in where you belong in twelve months and then more pins for each expected MQ until you reach your end goal of the optimal position.

Now develop a plan to influence each tier of the influence pyramid. Assign responsibility for each action item in the plan. Obtain the resources to implement and track each step of the plan.

CHAPTER SIX
The MQ Plan

The MQ plan uses the influence pyramid as a guide. Each tier has its actions that lead to positive results in influence, but don't forget that along the way you are generating sales, too. Influence has a much greater role than achieving a particular position in the Gartner Magic Quadrant.

Addressable Market

You are already selling to your addressable market of course. But how do you create influence? There are three important categories of activity.

Customer relations

As you gain customers enroll them in a community. This can take many forms. You need to build that sense of belonging, being part of something. Leverage the natural human tendency to congregate in like-minded groups with similar experiences. They all have you in common. Give them access to a portal. Let them contribute comments, product improvement suggestions, even complaints. Support the commenters, respond to the suggestions, and address the complaints. Identify the most prolific contributors to your community. Turn them into advocates. Do they also blog? Follow their blogs and comment when it is warranted. Yes, you are preaching to the choir, but what preacher doesn't?

Next, create a customer council made up of a representative slice of your customer base. Invite them to headquarters for a day-long meeting where you introduce them to your executives. Let them hear from the CEO on the company vision and the CTO on new product plans. Give them visibility into your organization. They get the benefit of mixing with their counterparts at different companies. Make sure your people are mixing with them too so that you can pick up on otherwise unvoiced problems--and address those problems by acknowledging them and presenting a plan to overcome them.

Brand building

Many tech firms ignore brand marketing. All of their marketing focus is on lead generation and channel marketing, but there is no greater payoff than creating name recognition and no greater missed opportunity than having zero name recognition. When I was sucked out of my nascent efforts to become an independent analyst by the CEO of Fortinet to become their Chief Marketing Officer, the number one problem they suffered was name recognition. Here was a company with 20,000 customers worldwide, 900 employees, and revenue over $120 million that had *no* name recognition. The sales team even had a name for the issue; they called it the Forti-who? problem. Every single sales call by any one of the 150 salespeople at Fortinet started with an introduction where they had to answer the question "Who is Fortinet?" That is the most expensive and wasteful brand awareness plan you can have. Like all marketing efforts you must measure brand awareness first to understand where you sit and be able to demonstrate success from any investment you make to improve name recognition.

Hire a market research firm to survey a representative segment of the base of the pyramid. How many can identify your company name and what you do? Then gear up your marketing, PR, and executives to increase that brand awareness. This is not a book on marketing but you know what to do to get your name out there. At the end of the day the goal is to change that first response when a sales rep cold-calls a prospect from "Who?" to "Oh yes, I've heard of you."

Channel development

Working with the channel is the third way to develop influence in the lower tier. Channel sales people talk to each other, your competitors, and sometimes even your potential customers. You can tell that I am somewhat jaded when it comes to the channel, especially in the United States. Frankly, the channel is greedy and lazy. They want the vendor to supply not just leads but closed deals where their only task is to get the paperwork, make sure the product ships, and collect the money. They would much rather hire one more person for the back office to process paperwork than another sales person to specialize in your product. That's okay though, you just have to realize that adding resellers and distributors does not magically produce more revenue. Play into their desires. Give them great margins (you have to to break them away from the entrenched incumbent in your space). Make their job easy. Give them done deals. Give them a piece of the support contract even though they won't ever talk to the customer again. (I told you I was jaded). If you help them succeed they will talk about you in a positive way. That's influence.

Social Networks

You have the ball rolling on getting the base of the pyramid to know who you are. Now start working social networks to ensure there is a constant stream of activity around what you do. You never want an analyst to search Twitter for mentions of your company and find the last Tweet dated six months ago. If no one is talking about your company you must be dead, right? Here is some guidance for now. There are lots of details in how to leverage Twitter, LinkedIn, and Facebook in the chapter on social networks.

Twitter

Get a corporate account and assign it to one or more people, probably in your marketing department. This is the Twitter ID that tweets company and industry news. It also re-Tweets the analysts that you are targeting. Then train your CEO and CTO how to use Twitter. Study the CEO of Zappos' use of Twitter for a template of how to do it right. After that, encourage, maybe even require, all company employees to have Twitter accounts. Give them a little training in how to use Twitter to contribute to the success of the company. This means that they will be re-Tweeting the corporate ID and the CEO's Tweets along with all of their normal Tweets about their favorite sports teams and what they had for breakfast. Of course they should be admonished not to Tweet about the bad day at the office.

LinkedIn

LinkedIn was primarily created as a networking tool and is often viewed as a danger because it is a powerful way to lose employees due to the heavy recruiting activity. But keep in mind that most journalists, customers, and yes, even analysts, are on LinkedIn already. The analysts that have discovered LinkedIn stop by to check up on your company. They can see the number of employees that are on LinkedIn. They can search for key contacts. They can even view reports that summarize which companies you hire from and where your employees go when they leave. Often they can identify the up-and-comers by seeing the exodus from a legacy vendor to a new vendor. Encourage your key execs and marketing people to post positive updates, news mentions, and industry developments to their LinkedIn feeds. It works a lot like Facebook but, thankfully, most updates are business related, not personal. I am not a fan of hooking Twitter accounts to LinkedIn. The updates get too chatty. Be selective in which Tweets you want to re-post to LinkedIn.

Facebook

Even after its IPO Facebook is struggling as a business tool. Because it was born as a way to keep in touch with friends and family, it is not built for business communication. You may want to look at Facebook ads though. Facebook ads are interesting because you can target people who work at particular companies. During the set up process you simply pick those companies. Unfortunately, many people do not identify themselves with their employer on Facebook; it's a personal tool to them. Go ahead and create branding ads and target them at your prospect list. The odds are slim that an analyst will see them but at least you will be targeting the base of the pyramid. You should also have a Facebook page. While analysts may not "like it" your customers will. After that, every time you post to your page they will see your updates in their news feed.

Wikipedia

Not a social network, of course. Wikipedia is a crowd sourced encyclopedia of all knowledge--or at least that is what it strives to be. Lots more on Wikipedia in a later chapter but for now:

Make sure you have a Wikipedia entry for your company. Populate your Wikipedia entry with facts about your company. Include a citation for every single statement you make.

Bloggers/Journalists

As you get higher up the pyramid, the more focused your activity gets. You begin to target particular bloggers, journalists, end-user influencers, and analysts. Most organizations are already set up to influence journalists. That is what your PR firm does. Luckily, many PR firms have jumped on the social networking bandwagon so you may already have activities in place to influence this tier.

In addition to the regular PR activity of press releases, follow up, story planting, press tours, etc., you should also:

-Identify key bloggers and journalists (often the same thing).

-Read every blog post by anyone on your target list.

-Use Google alerts to pick up on any blogger that mentions you, your product, your executives, or your industry sector.

-Make insightful useful comments to those posts.

-Tweet links to those posts and mention the blogger by name or Twitter ID. That way they will see your Tweet.

-Engage with the top bloggers in your space. Get to know them. Brief them. Take them out to dinner or meet them for breakfast at the next conference they attend. Better yet, have your CEO do this.

As I have said, analysts are info junkies. They spend most of their lives, when they are not on the phone, online. They have Google alerts set up on the companies they track. If they read a post about your company or sector they might see the comment you left. It is just one more touch point that helps to keep you at top of the analyst's mind.

A word about those comments. It is bad form to respond to a blog post with something like: "Our company does this too. You can buy our products at..." That is spam. Choose an ID that reflects your company name or brand and comment with substance. It is subtle but it is the only way to break through the shields the influencer erects when he/she sees a comment from a "marketer". Be real. Be a person.

CIOs at the Global 10,000

The CIOs (and IT directors) at the Global 10,000 enterprises are the primary influencers of analysts. They are the ones who provide the best data points for the analysts to squirrel away in their packed brains.

When I learned that one of the major Wall Street banks had completed their three year review of firewalls and selected Juniper over Check Point, I knew it was safe to move Juniper ahead of Check Point and Cisco in the Leaders Quadrant. Gartner does not do product evaluations. A VP of Research has not had hands-on experience with products for at least three years, possibly ten or fifteen. If a major organization makes a decision to switch vendors that is the best possible affirmation.

The point of targeting the Global 10,000 is that these are most likely to have relationships with Gartner. These late adaptors often fit into the "what does Gartner say?" group of IT decision makers. They are making buying decisions that will cost millions of dollars and that they will have to live with for many years. They feel they need Gartner's blessing to make any move. Where does that leave you? If you are placed low in the Magic Quadrant, during the inquiry call the analyst is going to ask questions of the CIO to determine if their needs match your strengths. If you are one of the few Leaders, the call to the analyst might not even happen since the CIO has a document to point to, one that was probably used to start the evaluation process in the first place.

Identify the IT executives that are already your customers who have a relationship with Gartner. All you have to do is ask. The sales team will play an important role in identifying these contacts. Invite that CIO or senior IT staffer to join your customer advisory board. CIOs go to a lot of conferences and meetings with their peers. You want to influence them to the point where they provide positive references to their counterparts at other companies and ultimately to the analyst.

Of course, the best way to turn a CIO into a fan is to fulfill your end of the bargain when they purchase your product. Demonstrate your world class support. Dedicate a sales engineer to that customer for the duration of the installation and beyond, if needed.

There is a story of a major Cisco customer in Chicago that was experiencing problems with a big install. The SE on the job took Friday afternoon off to head North fishing, and was unreachable. The customer's network was down and the CIO was livid. He went all the way to the top at Cisco to demand satisfaction. The SE was fired and the head of the Chicago office was fired. A team of Cisco engineers was assigned to the project to provide 24/7 coverage until all the problems were resolved. Cisco earned a customer for life and the CIO became one of their biggest fans. The story may be annecdotal but it illustrates a good point. Even if an install does not go smoothly you can still win over the CIO by simply being *responsive*.

Analysts

Most of this book is about influencing analysts. It is at this top tier that you should have the most focused effort. As a rule of thumb I usually advise startups that they do not need a dedicated analyst relations (AR) person until they hit about $50 million in revenue. Sometimes a vendor will be in a hot space that is getting a lot of attention from the analyst community. In that case it pays to assign that AR role, even if it is to one of the founders, at an earlier stage. But even without a dedicated AR person, you still need to brief the analysts to make them aware of your existence and often they will provide valuable guidance. Your PR firm can take on this role.

You should identify all of the analysts that cover your segment and schedule briefings with them at least once every six months. They should get your press releases. Please do not blast press releases to your entire cc list! Soon after starting IT-Harvest I received such a blast from an AR person at Waggener Edstrom (the firm that handles all of Microsoft's PR and AR work). As so often happens, she put the list of recipients in the cc field, not the bcc (blind copy) field. There were *three thousand* analysts and journalists on her list! Make sure to personally address each email sent to influencers, or use an email tool that *never* screws up.

If Gartner does not cover your space (CAD/CAM software for instance), you can still use most of the guidance below and in the rest of this book. You will just have to set your goals differently. You might target the Forrester Wave, the relevant IDC or Infonetics market spreadsheets, or just becoming the most frequently recommended vendor by a particular analyst--think Walt Mossberg and Apple.

Gartner Analysts

The rest of this book puts the meat on the bone of an analyst influence strategy. Specific tactics are revealed for addressing all of the ways you can interact with Gartner analysts: inquiries, briefings, analyst days (SAS), industry conferences, Gartner Summits, and Gartner's IT Symposium. In addition some guerrilla tactics are provided that might be game changers in your journey UP and to the RIGHT.

Now you have set your goal--the desired position of your company in the relevant Magic Quadrants. You have a plan--the tasks, responsibilities and resources. The next step is to implement the plan.

CHAPTER SEVEN
Finding The Influencers

Identifying influencers to target has an easy component and a more difficult component. It is relatively simple to identify who the analysts, journalists, bloggers, and experts are. It is much harder to measure their influence.

Let's start at the top and work our way down.

Analysts

Any analyst who has written about your space should be on your list. Use Google to find them. There are probably going to be new analysts covering your space every quarter. As new research is published keep track of the analysts who author it. Keep an eye out for independent analysts with a strong voice. They may not even be writing about your space but you may find them quoted often addressing what you do in the mainstream media. Also, build a list of other analysts at the same firm who play a supporting role to those who directly cover your space.

How do you judge an analyst's influence? Here are

some techniques that can help. First of all, the analyst or analysts that author your Magic Quadrant are, for the purposes of achieving your goal, the most influential. You will find that many Gartner analysts completely fail the influence measurements listed below. They may not talk to the press, they may not blog, they may completely avoid that "new-fangled social media garbage." But every September they may stand in front of 10,000 IT professionals at Symposium and read them the Gospel that defines buying patterns in your space for the next year.

Quotes

Do a Google News search on the analyst. Set the time frame for the previous 12 months. Historically, the most quoted Gartner analyst has been Avivah Litan. She covers credit card fraud which is a perpetually hot topic. As of this writing, Google shows 129 quotes for Litan in the past 12 months. Use that as a measure of extremely high influence. No matter the absolute number, by comparing the number of quotes for each analyst on your list you can get an idea for their relative influence. In the Guerrilla Techniques chapter you will see how you can impact the number of quotes an analyst gets... to your advantage.

Twitter score

Find out the Twitter ID of each analyst. Look at their Twitter account and note the number of followers they have. This can be misleading because the analysts may have applied some of the techniques I am going to share in the chapter on social media, but I doubt it. I have seen no evidence that any analyst (other than me) has figured Twitter out, so the number of followers an analyst has is a good measure that can be used to rank them. For a better score that takes into account number of Tweets, number of Re-Tweets, etc., check out the tool provided by Hubspot at tweet.grader.com

Klout

Klout.com is a great tool for measuring relative influence, at least on social media. It measures activity and connections on Twitter, Facebook, and LinkedIn.

You can also survey your customer base or the bottom of the influence pyramid to see what blogs they read and which analysts' names they recognize.

Bloggers

Google is your best tool to find bloggers. Search on relevant terms using the Google Blogs tool and set up alerts so that over time you build a list of influencers who touch on your category. You can apply the same techniques to measuring their influence. Don't be surprised to discover that bloggers are much more active on Twitter and other social media than the typical analyst. They will have thousands instead of hundreds of followers and they will Tweet frequently. This is how they drive traffic to their blogs. Their Klout and Hubspot scores will be higher too.

Journalists

Reporters have hard jobs. They are usually assigned to a "beat" and don't pay much attention to anything else. A journalist who covers your space, usually the tech beat, may not be a frequent influencer but when he or she does write about your particular category, they can have a marked impact. So identify those journalists, many at trade magazines and websites, who have written about your space before. As in traditional PR a good starting point for measuring influence is the gross readership of the publication. Obviously the *New York Times, Wall Street Journal, Financial Times*, or *USA Today* journalists are going to be very influential. If there is a single publication for your space, get to know all of the writers and editors there.

Create your master list of targeted influencers from the top of the pyramid (Gartner analysts) to the bottom (active end-users on Twitter and forums). In each category rank them in influence weighted for their influence on the Gartner analyst who authors your Magic Quadrant. Now apply your MQ plan to these influencers. Follow them and Re-Tweet them on Twitter. Brief the bloggers, journalists, and analysts.

In the next chapters we delve into the direct influence activities you will perform to engage the Gartner analysts, starting with the SAS day.

CHAPTER EIGHT
The SAS Day

The Strategic Advisory Service (SAS) is a product that Gartner makes available to vendors and end-user organizations. For vendors it is a day-long, bottom-up review of your products, markets, sales wins, and strategy with a key analyst (or more than one). For end-users it is a deep dive into either their technology practices and product selections or simply a briefing on the state of a particular technology category.

The SAS day is probably not the first of many ways you will engage with Gartner. It *is* the most powerful and pays the greatest dividends. This is, in part, where the pay-to-play myth arises. Sure, you have to pay for a SAS day, but you are not buying the analyst's opinion--you are buying his or her time. What you do with that time is up to you.

Let's talk about cost. Expect to pay about $12K plus travel expenses to get an analyst to spend a day on-site with you. If the analyst has to travel overseas you may have to pay for two days and business class airfare. But there are other ways to pay for a SAS day that can lower the out-of-pocket cost. Gartner's sales model is mostly direct. They employ account managers that have geographic and vertical responsibilities and inside sales reps housed in Fort Meyers, Florida, that work the phones. As a vendor you will probably work with a sales rep that focuses just on vendors. There are several regions around the world where there are Gartner "re-sellers"-- independent reps that have the whole territory. Alaska, Hawaii, and Israel are examples of such regions. Negotiate with your Gartner sales person to get the best deal. They have considerable flexibility. Most vendors will buy a package that includes access to the research in their area, inquiry privileges, a couple of tickets to Symposium, and one SAS day. This can reduce the cost of that SAS day but the overall cost can easily be over $30K. While you are negotiating a package you may want to try to get booth space at the particular Gartner Summit that covers your area or even at Symposium, but there are separate sales people for Gartner Events so your sales rep might not have much leeway to offer deals on events.

I have known startups, one headed by an ex-Gartner sales exec, who manage to purchase just SAS days. If you have only $12K to spend on Gartner this is the best idea, especially for a young company not yet on a Magic Quadrant.

There are two sides of the SAS day. What information and impression you convey to the analyst, and the advice the analyst provides. Do not discount that advice. There are ineffective analysts and there are good analysts. The good analysts have seen dozens of companies at the same stage as yours. They have participated in similar deep dives with them. They have seen what worked and what failed miserably. Listen to what they say. Ask good questions. This is your chance to learn from their experience. But I am getting ahead of myself. First we have to plan for the SAS day.

While I am taking the SAS day out of order because of its importance, you must prepare for it with briefings and inquiries. By the time the analyst shows up in your lobby she should be well briefed on who you are and what products you sell. Your entire company should be prepped for the meeting. So, follow this process:

Get on the analyst's calendar. This can be tough. When I was at Gartner I participated in about forty five SAS and speaking engagement days a year. (I once did three in two days, but that is another story.) There were analysts who far exceeded my travel days. Enlist your Gartner sales rep to get a date that works for you and the analyst. Expect it to be at least three months out, but check because the analyst may be in your area sooner and will jump at the chance to limit his days away from home by avoiding one more trip.

Once a date is set make sure to schedule a briefing before the SAS day. If the analyst has been recently briefed by you keep this one short. Just cover the agenda for the day. There are three goals to this call:

1. Set expectations for what you want from the analyst. A presentation on the competitive landscape? The key criteria in the MQ? The CIO perspective? A critique of your go-to-market strategy?

2. The schedule for the day. (See below)

3. An invitation to dinner the night before the SAS day.

That's right. You are going to ask the analyst out to dinner. You have to do that before the analyst makes his travel arrangements, otherwise he is going to make plans for taking an overseas call from his hotel room, or present a webinar, or go to dinner with a friend in the area or an enterprise the Gartner sales rep is trying to close. This is your chance to build a closer relationship between the analyst and your key execs, preferably your CEO. Oh, and ask the analyst about any food preferences or things to avoid.

The dinner can be just a tete-a-tete between your CEO and the analyst or you can decide to invite more people. Keep it to six max. You don't have to go to the best restaurant in town but it should be an interesting one. Gartner analysts have seen it all and as a rule are gourmands. The other attendees should include the primary contact person (usually the AR person), the VP of sales, the CTO, the CEO, and possibly a happy customer. Do not turn the dinner into a pitch. It is purely a social event to build connections between key company representatives and the analyst. Analysts are talkers (otherwise they would not be analysts) and they have vast interests outside the segments they cover. Get to know those interests. One more word, don't attempt to be too social. Exercise restraint in serving the fine wine and drinks. You want everyone to be in top shape in the morning.

Preparing for the SAS day

First, you must prep anyone who is going to participate in the SAS day. Explain to them the overall strategy (which you have, right?) for engaging Gartner. Provide a detailed bio of the analyst and copies of recent Notes she has written. If you have a particularly confrontational CTO or other stakeholder you may want to have a substitute. There are going to be moments during the SAS day when the adrenaline flows. You don't want those moments to be a heated argument that puts the analyst on the defensive. They will remember those moments for the rest of their career and will live to prove themselves right. You want those electricity-charged moments to be when the analyst "gets it," when something clicks and he sees what you are doing and why it will work. You can't necessarily create that moment, but you can avoid the other kind. Other things to include in the prep:

-Make a list of words to avoid. At all costs never engage in "marketing speak." Scrub all your slide decks of words like 'synergy' and 'holistic' (some Gartner analysts play a mental game where they replace 'holistic' with 'imaginary'--it's fun.)

-Never even come close to providing an MQ analysis. Don't use the phrases "ability to execute" or "completeness of vision."

-Assign key questions to each participant. They can be broad ones--"where do you think the market is headed?" or specific--"what are the top three log management tools with which we should integrate?"

-Give the analyst data. Analysts love data.

-Next come up with an agenda. Use this one as a starting place:

Agenda

8:00 AM Introductions

8:30 Our company vision presented by the CEO

9:30 Deep dive on product 1, CTO or product manager

10:30 Deep dive on product 2, CTO or product manager

11:30 Demo of product in development

12:00 Lunch brought in, customer presentation

1:30 Sales strategy and deep dive on results, VP World Wide Sales

2:30 Call-in from VP of EMEA

3:30 Presentation from analyst on state of the industry

4:00 Wrap up

The lunch presentation from an influential customer is one of the most important aspects of the day. The customer's presentation should follow this format: The problem we had, how we chose this vendor, how the problem was solved. The analyst will be completely in his/her element for this. Don't forget she/he does hundreds of such meetings (by phone) a year. They will pepper your customer with questions. Pay attention! Note those questions. You are getting an inside glance at how the analyst conducts an inquiry.

The analyst presentation can be scheduled earlier in the day but I find if it is the last session you can judge how much you impacted the analyst by how he fits you into the story. He will stress the areas where you match his vision and where you are at odds.

Wrap up early. Give the poor guy a break.

Email the agenda directly to the analyst. This may be your first chance to jump past the Gartner gatekeepers who protect the analyst from direct contact with vendors. His email address is first.last@gartner.com if you do not have it already.

Now that you have an agenda, put together the presentations. You should have a rehearsal to make sure that each presenter covers new material. I have seen the same presentation three times in one SAS day. Follow best practices in presentations: avoid bullet points, use stories to illustrate points, and provide lots of data.

An important point about having other analysts'

quotes in presentations: don't do it. If you do you should not be surprised if you hear a snort of derision when you flash the quote from the IDC or Forrester analyst that says you are the leader in the space. They won't even recognize the dude's name unless he used to be a Gartner analyst, and that is even worse. He couldn't take the heat, so he left. Or he tried to get rich by joining a vendor and it went south. Gartner would not take him back so he had to settle for the second string analyst firm. That said, if you have a slide of industry recognition and achievements it is okay to leave another analyst firm there. Just avoid those quotes. A good demo will leave the analyst with the impression that he could use your product himself. He should be able to visualize his clients using your product.

The day of

Just a few points for the SAS day. Strive to make logistics easy for the analyst. Offer to pick him up from the hotel. Hire a car to take him to the airport at the end of the day. If the analyst has a rental car make sure he has explicit directions from the hotel to your office.

When the analyst arrives make sure the receptionist is expecting him. If you have a sign that welcomes guests put a welcome message on it. You don't have a receptionist? That is a problem. There is nothing that creates as bad an impression as arriving in a bare lobby with an empty desk and notice to dial extension *781 to reach someone. Despite the hours you have spent preparing for this meeting and the months you have spent getting to know the analyst he will have forgotten your name. He won't know who to ask for. He will wonder if he came to the right address. That first impression is an important one. The analyst has already drawn conclusions from your location. Sun Prairie, Wisconsin? Drive around to the shipping dock to get in? What kind of an outfit is this anyway? Don't exacerbate the bad impression with your office. Is your company name clearly visible on the building? Is your company listed in the building directory? Get someone to occupy the front desk. I know that receptionists are not new-tech. When your investors visit they appreciate the Spartan look, but an analyst is looking for signs of prosperity, professionalism, and efficiency.

When the receptionist has greeted the analyst and called him in, go to get him right away. Give him the chef's tour on the way to the meeting room. It's early so you may want to make sure that everyone is at their desks on the day of the SAS. That may be a problem with your developers. Just make sure the analyst is not exposed to rows of cubicles with no one in them. You are trying to impress him with the excitement and energy of your company, not with the number of desks you have. If the analyst happens to know someone in your organization from a previous work experience (highly likely) make sure to walk him by and let them greet each other.

Now lead him to your best conference room. Don't make excuses for holding the meeting in a corner of the cafeteria because the CEO is meeting with the board or an important sales meeting is going on (yes, these are all examples from SAS days I have been on.) Have coffee, tea or RedBull ready in the meeting room. (You *do* know what the analyst's favorite morning beverage is don't you?) Have a supply of caloric fuel handy too. Keep in mind that analysts either eat unwisely or they are very health conscious depending on how long they been an analyst. The senior analysts are trying to lose weight and stay fit, so offering them baked goods is a problem. Besides, you don't want them falling asleep from a carb coma. At least have yogurt and fruit on hand in addition to the usual bagels and cream cheese.

Now the meeting kicks off with the CEO's presentation. Does it have to be the CEO? In most cases, yes. Your CEO is, I hope, the representative of the company's vision. In addition to the instant respect the CEO commands for his accomplishments, perhaps with several previous successful companies the analyst is familiar with, one of your major tasks is to build rapport between the CEO and the analyst. The top CEOs in technology pay considerable attention to Gartner analysts. Bill Gates, and many other CEOs have traveled to Stamford for day-long sessions. When I was with Gartner I attended sessions with the CEOs of Cisco and Symantec. They were engaged and knowledgable about my coverage area and writing. John Chambers could even quote my own research to me. The only case where it makes sense *not* to have the CEO present is if you are a division of a very large organization and the CEO is not really identified with your products. I would not expect the CEO of Intel to show up at a SAS day to discuss McAfee, for instance.

As you work your way through the day get as much as you can from the analyst. Ask questions. Take notes. And oh yes, don't be put off by one particular type of analyst, the one who shows up carrying nothing. No bag, no computer, no iPad, no pad of paper. No note taking. He is the expert and he will remember everything you say. Well, that is the impression he is trying to convey anyway. Provide him with hard copies of the presentations and a pen.

This is a good time to talk about confidentiality. Every vendor wants the analyst to sign a Non-Disclosure Agreement (NDA). This does not happen. Somewhere buried in your contract with Gartner is language regarding confidentiality, or so your sales rep will tell you. I have not seen it, but that is all you are going to get. Gartner analysts do not sign NDAs, but they also are trained from years of practice not to reveal confidential data. They may have just come from a SAS day with your competitor but you will never know it. The analyst will not reveal what your competitors are doing just as the analyst will not reveal what you are doing to your competitors. If you are working on a top secret project, planning an acquisition, or getting ready to sell out, DO NOT reveal it to the analyst. If you are publicly traded, follow all the regulations that bar revealing non-public information. As a rule analysts do not own stock in companies they track, but you do not want them telling their investor clients inside information. Everyone will get in trouble.

Follow up

Send a thank you note with any promised documentation to the analyst within a few days of the SAS. If any action items came out of the meeting record them in this email.

Planning the next SAS day

Any more than one SAS day a year is probably overkill. The second SAS day is important for one crucial thing: to demonstrate that you listened to the analyst's advice and took action. If the analyst suggested you open an office in Europe and you have, make that a key point in the next session. If she provided insights on product positioning and you followed through on them, highlight that too. I am not suggesting that you put 100% trust in the analyst and do everything they say. At the end of the day you know your market and customer requirements better than any analyst. I am just saying that you should demonstrate that you heard the analyst at the last session and took action based on their advice. There is no stronger way to influence an analyst directly than to follow their advice and give them credit for it.

It works like this: If the analyst tells you to do X, Y, and Z to get in the Leaders Quadrant, do X, Y, and Z, and demonstrate that you did so on the analyst's advice. Boom, you are in the Leaders Quadrant. It's as simple as that. I saw one vendor do this with great effect. The Gartner analyst tore the vendor up at a SAS day, told them everything they were doing wrong and predicted their immediate demise unless they took corrective action to fit into his vision for the market. They listened carefully and six months later convinced him that they had done everything he had suggested. They became the top Leader in the next Magic Quadrant.

You've heard that perception is everything? Well, there is some truth in that. Yes, the analyst can provide great advice, but he can be completely off base too. But it is a losing game to try to convince an analyst that he is wrong. You do what you need to do to win in the market place. Just apply your influence strategy to convince the analyst that you are complying with their vision at the same time.

I don't know if the interview process to become an analyst is still the same at Gartner as it was in 2000, but let me provide some insight about it to highlight why it is so hard to convince an analyst he is wrong. The candidate is provided with several themes to write on. On the day of the interview, he sits down in a little room under the stairwell in the Stamford headquarters and in two hours writes a research note.

Then he is led to a conference room with six or more analysts present, including the hiring manager. He proceeds to defend his conclusions against a group of experts who tear down his ideas. If he backs down in any way he is not offered a position. End of story. You see why analysts are so stubborn? They are *selected* for stubbornness!

Just to be absolutely clear. I am not suggesting that you blindly do whatever the analyst tells you. I am suggesting that you align whatever you do with the analyst's expectations.

CHAPTER NINE
The Analyst Inquiry

If you are a Gartner client, a critical privilege you have paid for is the analyst inquiry. This is the same service that end-user customers of Gartner use to get answers to questions regarding technology trends and product selection, but in your case you are going to get answers to questions on your market, what those end-users are looking for, and of course, what the analyst is looking for in vendors that appear in the Magic Quadrant.

You should schedule inquiries often enough to remind the analyst that you are there. You can request a particular analyst but sometimes you will be foisted off on a substitute. No problem, get to know as many analysts as you can. Within Gartner anyway, analysts do talk to each other. You should think of reasons to schedule inquiries with other analysts on a regular basis. Keep the activity level high. Take advantage of the service you paid for.

To schedule an inquiry you email inquiry@gartner.com and eventually you will be assigned a time on the analyst's calendar. Be prepared.

While the inquiry is *not* a mini-briefing, you still want to use it to influence the analyst. Ask questions that indicate where you are in your development stage. Is it about expansion in EMEA or AsiaPac? Suggestions for a CMO? Short list for acquisitions? Due diligence on an acquisition? All of these are very telling questions. Or perhaps you want the analyst's feedback on a marketing message? That is not super-subtle, but still legitimate. The key is to ask questions. My four years at Gartner left me with an odd ability (or disability depending on the situation.) I am programmed to answer questions. I can stare at a blank Wordpress form for ages trying to think of something wise and pithy to say, but if a journalist or client sends me a question I can rattle off an essay in reply. Gartner analysts spend their days answering questions. Many are like me and are pre-programmed to provide answers in 15 minute mini-lectures. That way there is only time to cover two questions in half an hour. So if you ask an analyst about a new segment you are getting into, be prepared for a long answer.

Be casual during the inquiry. The analyst is there to help you. It's his job. Break down the barriers. He freezes up when he sees he is getting on a call with a vendor. He knows what you are up to. Heck, by the time you have read this book, so has he! So set him at his ease. Tell him right up front that you are calling because you have a question. Break the ice. Be cognizant of the fact that he just had to beg off a call with another client because he "had a hard stop at the top of the hour" and he is going to hop on another call as soon as he hangs up with you. So ask your question, get his answer and hop off. If you give him back ten minutes to take a break, check email, or grab a hot coffee he is going to be grateful and there will be less dread the next time you call.

Here are some more legitimate excuses to schedule an inquiry:

-M&A activity in your space or an adjacent space that could impact you

-Questions about product strategy

-Due diligence on a marketing or AR hire

-Due diligence on hiring a PR or AR firm (The PR firms do this to you, you know. They schedule calls with the analysts to figure out what you are doing wrong with your AR program so they can demonstrate how tight they are with the analysts when they pitch you.)

-The prep call before the SAS day or speaking engagement/road show you are doing with the analyst. (Don't get all finicky on the analyst. You get what you get. Don't expect a lot of modification to the standard presentation if you have engaged them for speaking.)

The analyst inquiry is your chance to get value out of your Gartner relationship. During the analyst *briefing* you will work you magic to influence the analyst.

CHAPTER TEN
The Analyst Briefing

It does not cost anything to brief an analyst. A lot of vendors don't realize this. The savvy ones do. The vetting process is more stringent than for an inquiry. You have to fill out a briefing request and send it in. You should know beforehand which analysts you want on the call; if you appeal to more than one, you may get several on the call. A briefing is a rare opportunity to get a full hour of an analyst's time, but do not read a bunch of bullet points to an analyst. Don't forget she has a full work load. If you don't keep her engaged she will be doing email and filling in her report from the previous call.

Typically you will have the AR person and a product person on the phone. The more senior the product person, the better. The CEO is even better if you are still a single product vendor. No matter who it is, they should be good at briefings. That means conversant with the product and used to handling questions and objections ("That's a great question, we have thought long and hard about that and here is what we came up with.")

Just as I described in the section on SAS days, the presentations should be professional. Not a lot of bullet points but lots of data. And keep the number of slides down. You try sitting through four to six briefings a day and see how you feel at the end of a day of slide presentations.

Now, some pointed advice on those slide presentations. Send your slides to the analyst beforehand. Do not even bother scheduling a Webex or other online presentation. The analyst is not necessarily sitting at her desk. She may be at the gate waiting for a flight or in a hotel room with no Internet access . You will see why the analyst likes to have the slides as soon as you start the presentation. She will interrupt to ask you to skip ahead to what you do. She will stipulate the existence of the problem. No need to go through the slide with the graph that goes up exponentially to the right, or the slide with the headlines from the papers, or the survey results that demonstrate nine out of ten CIOs agree... If you do include those slides be prepared for that interruption. It is the analyst's favorite trick. But it is not spiteful, she has seen all those slides a hundred times. She has created slides like that and even includes them in her own presentations. You are talking to the expert on the problem and the solution. Get to your solution. I recommend starting out with the 'who we are' slide that lists the top salient points. Who are your founders/key people? Where are you located? What do you do? How big are you (sales, revenue, etc.)? Let her pigeonhole you. It's the way an analyst's brain works. It has to be that way considering the amount of data and the number of vendors she talks to. The very next slide should be a big, beautiful picture of your product. If it is a hardware product this is great. If it is software or a service it is harder. Figure that out. You will need that picture for lots of other reasons anyway.

Now dive into how your product works: what components, what features, speeds, and feeds. Analysts love data. Have I said that before?

Pay attention to the questions the analyst poses. Answer honestly and professionally.

By way of example, let me tell you about the briefing from hell. A very big technology company (and a very big Gartner client) scheduled a briefing with four analysts in the security group to introduce them to the huge effort they were launching in the security space: security professional services. We got on the call and were exposed to a seventy page PowerPoint. It went on, and on, and on. There was no data, only bullet points about how well positioned the company was to offer consulting services. The four analysts were all on AOL Instant Messenger and our chat messages were less than complimentary. We colluded on who would ask what question to trip them up. We took turns putting ourselves on mute and getting up to go to the bathroom. It was a miserable and memorable moment. From that time on I refused to have anything to do with that vendor. I would not take calls from them and I made sure I was not available for their big analyst day or SAS engagements. Don't be that vendor. I never heard anything more of their professional services effort. It probably never got off the ground--they killed it with a PowerPoint presentation.

Every briefing should accomplish four goals:

1. Build a relationship
2. Form the overall opinion of your company
3. Gather intelligence on what the analyst is looking for
4. Plant a tagline in the analyst's brain

Build a relationship

Every interaction with the analyst builds on your relationship but the briefing is a structured opportunity to establish a communication bond. It is important to identify who is going to represent the company to the analyst. Contact consistency is key. If a different person briefs the analyst each time, they are not going to know anyone at your company at all. There are two separate bonds to create. The bond with the AR person and the bond with the product person.

The AR person is going to quickly get on a first-name basis with the analyst. She/he is the communicator, one who knows the company's message, people, and business, but not necessarily the ins and outs of the product. Not being technical is fine. The analyst does not expect the AR person to answer questions on product details, but the AR person is an excellent facilitator. This is the person who arranges all the briefings and inquiries and is on all the calls. If the analyst ever has a question, you want him to feel he can reach out directly by email, and eventually, phone the AR person. The AR person must get back to him as quickly as possible with the answer. Always cite the source when doing so. Mention by name the CEO, CTO, or product specialist, that provides the answer. Always build on the analyst's understanding of who your company is.

The AR person must attend events at which the key analysts are present. Build on the relationship by associating a face/personality with the name and voice on the phone. Schedule a breakfast meeting to include the AR person, the analyst, and the CEO or product specialist.

Get to know the analyst. What are his interests? He will have a lot. I have found that analysts may not be the warmest creatures but they have varied interests and usually more than one area of expertise. He may be a marathon runner, or skier, or engage in adventure travel. He may be a ham radio enthusiast, or collector of some arcane art objects. He may dream of being a cooper. (I am thinking of an analyst friend whose dream of making barrels coincides with my interest in distilling whiskey.)

Analyst personalities come in all types. Some are aloof, some are full of themselves, some are meek and nerdy. For the most part they do not excel at people skills. If they did, they probably would have become managers or executives. When getting to know an analyst keep in mind that all analysts are experts, and they know it. They are extremely confident on their home turf--their area of expertise. That is why they respond so well to questions. They know the answers and they revel in providing them. Often that confidence leaks over into other fields that they are not experts in: politics, health, the economy. Continue to feed their need and ask questions about those topics as well.

There is a certain class of analysts who treats vendors with scorn. I think it is because they became analysts before they were experts in a field. For a period in the late '90s Gartner experimented with hiring writers and journalists, sometimes right out of school. The idea was that as the company grew they would not be able to afford to hire the experts in every field. They wanted to create a business model that did not rely on finding and retaining rockstars. After all, having the Gartner Analyst title should be enough to establish the credentials of an analyst. Of course, since writing and communicating are such important qualities for an analyst many of these recruits turned into superb analysts. But along the way, many of them picked up on the wrong attitudes. Analysts are selected for stubbornness as I pointed out, and they are trained to be contrarians--curmudgeons. When they are new to Gartner they sit in on a lot of analyst calls and briefings to learn the ropes. When they see the senior analyst being harsh to a vendor they begin to assume that is what makes a good analyst. And, let's face it, the most controversial and reputation-building successes an analyst may be known for is his or her criticism of a market-leading vendor. The novice picks up on this and thinks that vendor bashing is the essence of being an analyst. In truth, this is very wrong. A senior analyst who came from industry realizes that the space they cover was created by vendors. All of the innovation and forward movement comes from vendors. Because, after all, the vendors are the only ones that have *more* contact with end-users than the analysts do. Their products are the result of many iterations of responding to customer requests for modifications or feature enhancement. Savvy analysts will still beat up the vendors, but will exhibit much more respect than the younger breed of analyst.

If your analyst is one of these vendor-bashers, be comforted that the rest of the vendors in your space get the same harsh treatment. You just have to do a better job of managing your analyst than your competitors.

A word of warning. A bond between an analyst and an AR person is fungible. The AR person can take the relationship with them if they are wooed away by a competitor. So show some love to this key person. He or she has a hard job that often goes unrecognized. Demonstrate that recognition. And NEVER pin responsibility for missing a target in Magic Quadrant placement on the Analyst Relations person. Executing on the MQ strategy is the responsibility of the whole organization.

Oh, and if *you* are the AR person, the immediate supervisor, the head of corporate communications, or the CMO, NEVER commit to a particular goal. You can influence your placement on the Magic Quadrant. You cannot guarantee it.

During briefings is when you also build the connection between the analyst and your product expert. Your expert may be the technical founder of your company if you are still small and growing, or it may be the product engineer or manager if you are a large established firm. It should *not* be the product marketing person. It has to be someone who works on developing the product, who knows the code it is written in, who works with customers on product issues, in short the technical owner of the product. This person will probably be more technical than the analyst and thus command respect. If he or she is also a well-known name in the industry from previous successes, or work in the open source community, all the better.

Make sure the product expert understands the complete strategy for analyst influence. Share the goal and the plan. Get him or her to understand the importance of analyst influence. Give him a copy of this book. Stress that there are things that can be learned from the analyst.

The product expert should be shepherded by the AR contact who will work to create opportunities to strengthen the bond with the analyst. Any white papers the product expert has written, or videos he/she has produced, should be shared with the analyst. The more the expert can teach the analyst the better. The AR person will arrange the breakfast or dinner with the analyst at conferences. The product expert will convey the excitement of what he/she is working on.

If the product expert is not a fluid communicator that is okay. Certainly fluidity and comfort comes with practice, maybe a little training, but the analyst will cut him some slack. They deal with geeks within their client base all the time.

Form the overall opinion of your company

The second purpose of the briefing is to convey a solid understanding of what your company is (ability to execute) and what your company does (completeness of vision). This might be hard if you are HP or Yahoo! right now. If the company is not even sure of where they are heading and what business they are in, the analyst will pick up on that. If you have a complicated message and a complicated go-to-market strategy, simplify. Make the image of your company easy to fit into the Magic Quadrant you are targeting.

By way of illustration: your company has a complete suite of office productivity tools, from word processing to financial planning to integrated voice-text-video. The analyst, however, only covers word processors and is gathering data for the next MQ on word processors. Don't depict your company as one that has dozens of perfectly integrated tools of which word processing is a small part. Paint your company as a word processing company that has built dozens of ancillary products that feed into the word processor. See what that does? Your disjointed scope is transformed into demonstrable completeness of vision!

This example may seem like a stretch on my part to make a point. But talk to Fortinet if you want a real world example. They built a new security platform that is not only a firewall, but incorporates the features of products that reside in as many as eight different Magic Quadrants. When they make a pitch to get included in the MQ on Secure Web Gateways (the devices that prevent you from going to malicious or inappropriate web sites from work) they are told "only purpose-built Secure Web Gateways are allowed in the MQ. You have a multi-purpose device so it can't be included." Imagine the frustration. Fortinet has more Secure Web Gateways deployed than any of the vendors in the MQ, but is not included!

Gather intelligence on what the analyst is looking for. It is during the briefing that you are going to be exposed to how the analyst thinks about the space. Try to understand that as clearly as you can. Ask questions for clarity. This intelligence is going to inform all of your future communication with the analyst. She thinks that growth in number of re-sellers is a key indicator of ability to execute? Make sure she knows about every major re-seller you sign up and the upward trend in numbers of re-sellers. Ask her to define completeness of vision. Is it a spread of products across consumer-SMB-Enterprise? Is it a particular feature? A cloud strategy? Scalability? Your competitors who are already in the Leaders Quadrant should have all the qualities she mentions. If they don't, ask how they became Leaders. Take what you learn and stress these areas of development in future briefings. If you are missing one of the requirements that demonstrate completeness of vision, come up with a strategy to get there. This is vision after all, you don't necessarily have to have the feature--just the plan to get there.

Plant a tagline in the analyst's brain

Have you seen the movie "Inception"? Leonardo DeCaprio is challenged to take on the hardest task of all: plant an idea in someone's head that he thinks is his own. That is what you have to do in the briefing, without the benefit of a dream-making machine. Start small with implanting a tag line. I can tell you that by the end of a busy week of briefings I cannot remember what the vendor I talked to on Monday even does without referring to my notes. At the minimum you want to implant a memory in the analyst's brain of who you are (your company name) and what you do.

"We are iKangaru, the marsupial tracking software company." In the strange way the world works, the very next week a Gartner client will call to inquire about marsupial tracking software. If you have done your job the analyst will spend half an hour talking about your products.

That's the easy part; the next task is much more difficult. You want to plant the seed of what makes you different. What about your company might force the analyst to re-think his own assumptions about completeness of vision in his MQ? "We are the only marsupial tracking company to realize that all marsupials have pouches." If you accomplish this you are the de-facto visionary. Now all you have to work on is ability to execute.

Think long and hard about what you want to surgically implant in the analyst's brain. Going back in and removing it or replacing it may be impossible. Ideas are like cancer; they grow.

The best possible way to implant an idea is to create that "inception" moment. Give the analyst all the information she needs to come up with the idea on her own. Often you will be able to tell. The tone of the briefing changes. The analyst "gets it". She starts asking clarifying questions. If you are a client she may even state it for you: "Hey, you are the only vendor in the space that actually uses pouches for marsupial tracking!" Your job is done.

I have had this strategy expertly played on me recently. Nine years ago, when I was at Gartner, I was responsible for the Intrusion Detection (IDS) Magic Quadrant. Three different startups briefed me in the same month. Their message was: IDS does not work, Intrusion Prevention (IPS) is what is needed. I was skeptical at first, but they kept hammering at me, in particular the CTO of one firm. I began to dig into how IDS was being used within the Gartner client base. Everyone deployed IDS, but they all ignored the millions of alerts it generated. It was expensive and so unmanageable that no one managed it. The upshot was that I canceled the IDS MQ and began the IPS Magic Quadrant, leaving it to my replacement when I left Gartner. Two years ago the same CTO from that IPS vendor had moved on and began reaching out to me. We had dinner whenever I was in town. He was on to something big he would tell me. He was planting the seed. Last year he got funding and hired the AR person from his previous company and set up a briefing. Note that he went into the first briefing with an established dual bond. He was the product expert bond, she was the AR bond. Half-way through the briefing it clicked. They were re-inventing another space. I could write that the legacy technology was dead, their new approach was the way to go. You could feel the high-fives over the phone. They had succeeded in implanting an idea in my head, and I was the one to connect the dots. That is masterful use of a briefing.

CHAPTER ELEVEN
The Drop-By Briefing

There is a special case of the briefing that you won't find explained anywhere else. That is the impromptu briefing, or as I call it, the drop-by briefing. You have to work to make these happen. Basically, find out where the analyst lives and drop him or her a note the week before you are going to be in town.

The set up

You know how it works: "Hey, I am going to be passing through your neck of the woods next week. Do you have any availability to meet? I have something to show you." This has got to come from the product expert, not the AR person. The AR person might be the instigator pulling the strings, but the product expert is the sole participant. Ideally it comes from the CEO/founder of the company. Even the busiest CEO of a Fortune 500 technology company will acknowledge that pushing the MQ Plan forward is a good use of her time. Make sure that the analyst picks up on the fact that this is a meet and greet, *not* a job interview. He gets a lot of those. If the analyst agrees, you want him to know that he will be wearing his analyst hat--this is business as usual.

It may take a lot of "trips through town" to get this meeting. If the analyst lives someplace out of the way, of course, you won't be able to claim that you have that much business in Edmonton. In that case be more explicit: "I think it is extremely important that we get to know one another. You name a time and place and I will be there." I have had this experience four times, always with a CEO, and in every case the vendor was not a Gartner client. Each time the CEO had had previous industry experience and knew the value of analyst interactions. One CEO flew up with his technical founder and they set up a wifi hotspot in my local Starbucks with three different wireless sources and a sensor to detect hacking. Obviously, the memory has stuck with me. The CEO eventually sold the company to Motorola and is now on his fifth or sixth venture. Even at that impromptu briefing/demo at Starbucks he was wealthy from a previous successful venture. Never think that wooing analysts is beneath your position. Another CEO was in Detroit to talk to an auto company. He called ahead the day before and offered to take me to the best restaurant in town. I had to ask around to figure out which restaurant that was. It was an amazing meal and a great meeting with someone who has become a lifelong friend. And thanks to that meeting I had discovered the perfect place to propose to my wife-to-be a year later.

The briefing itself can take several forms. It could be a first introduction to the vendor as they launch, or it could be as the vendor introduces its first product in the space the analyst covers. It could be to pre-announce an acquisition or the sale of the company. It could be a demo, if the product fits on a laptop. Or it could simply be a bond building experience. Your best bet is to shoot for coffee during the day. Analysts don't have many evenings that they get to spend with their families.

The follow-through

Follow up with the analyst. If you asked for something during your drop-by briefing, like a formal briefing, make that happen. If the analyst asked for more information, get it to him. It's a bit of a dating game. Think ahead to your next meeting and set the stage for it.

CHAPTER TWELVE
The Summit

Gartner has a large events business. In addition to the massive IT Symposium, covered in the next chapter, they have smaller conferences throughout the year that focus on specialized industry segments. Security, Enterprise Architecture, and the carry over Meta Group Catalyst Conferences are a few of them. Go to www.gartner.com/technology/events to find which of the forty five conferences best serves your space.

Even while I was at Gartner I would recommend Gartner events as the best conference for vendors to spend money on. If, that is, you are targeting the medium to large enterprise. Don't forget Gartner's client base and focus. If you do share a common target market then you will not find another venue that presents such a target-rich environment for prospects. Gartner events are very expensive to attend so only serious IT buyers attend. Few, if any, students show up and there are only a smattering of journalists. It pays to have a booth at a Gartner event regardless of your MQ plan.

But the Gartner event is a valuable opportunity to push your analyst influence strategy forward. Here are the elements of a Gartner conference that you can leverage.

One-on-ones

The dreaded one-on-one space is usually set up in a hotel ballroom with knock down booths arranged in an institutional rat-maze. Dreaded, because every analyst is required to make time for one-on-ones and may face several hours of back-to-back half hour sessions with end-user clients and vendors. They may be dehydrated from the night before. They may be thinking about their presentation coming up in an hour. I have never met an analyst who likes the one-on-one sessions. They are mentally grueling sessions and most analysts try, but fail, to wiggle out of them. With that said, these sessions can be an opportunity to brief the analyst on something that is easier to do in person than on the phone. Whatever you do, make sure you are not wasting the analyst's time. Do not bring a Power Point to walk through in excruciating detail. A quick demo of a product feature is a good use of your allotted time. You could review a strategy document. Or you could simply take the opportunity to introduce the analyst to a key member of your team. The AR person must be at this meeting. The one thing the meeting should accomplish is to reinforce the tagline or idea that you are working diligently to implant in the analyst's brain. Repeat it in three different ways during the course of the 20 minutes. Yes, 20. Don't take the full 30 minutes. Every 30 minutes someone will be ringing chimes to alert the groups huddled in the cubicles to end their sessions and get on to the next one. Adult musical chairs. You sign up for one-on-ones online before the conference or at the desk outside the room. If you get the last slot in an analyst's schedule, for sure cut your session short. He will be grateful for the opportunity to escape early and head back to his room to chill out before his next duty. I have even had AR people who were particularly sympathetic grab that slot and then show up to tell me they did not really need a one-on-one but thought I could use the relief. I was truly grateful for that gift of 30 minutes.

Sponsorships

Your Gartner events sales person will be glad to sell you various sponsorships. There are the usual Silver/Gold/Platinum slots with signage and special notice on the web page and conference marketing material. There are lunches and dinners to sponsor. You can even sponsor the welcome reception the first night. All of these are large investments. Their highest value is when you are struggling to convince the analysts that you are real. If they continue to think of you as a small startup even though you have grown to 150 people and are doubling in size every year, now is the time to change their perception by sponsoring their event. Don't forget that the investment pays short-term dividends based on the sales opportunities and brand recognition you will be generating with the base of the pyramid as well as the CIOs who attend. Ensure that your sales team is represented in force. You don't want your marketing and AR people talking to buyers, you want your rainmakers talking to buyers. In many cases a single sale to a CIO that arises from a Gartner event will justify everything you spend on the event. Plus you will have acquired a customer who is a Gartner client, someone at the top of the Influence Pyramid. You know what to do with that.

Analyst presentations

Make sure you have enough people present to attend the analyst's presentations. You have to be in the room at every one of these. It is the polite thing to do. This is the big time for the analyst (even more so for Symposium, although not all analysts in a space go to Symposium). They have sweated to prepare a slide presentation. They have rehearsed to ensure an entertaining experience (the good ones have). If they know you are at the show (they just saw you in the one-on-ones or in your booth) and you are not in the audience, what does that say about your interest in what they have to say? How do they know you are in the room or not? You make sure they know. You tell them you are going to make a point of being there. You "bump into" them on the way into the room. Or you are sitting in front, rapt with attention. It is important that the analyst knows you are in the room because you are subtly pressuring the analyst to be polite when he mentions your company or product. He might not include you in his presentation, but he will probably walk through the MQ and your presence in the audience may induce him to mention you favorably, or at least avoid trashing you. If you have done something newsworthy recently he will mention that. If you are an up-and-comer he will mention that. If you have been deemed a "cool company of the year" he will mention it. But if you are not there he may say something snide or demeaning about your company. The last thing you want is for the analyst to lump you in with "the rest of the ankle biters down here in the Niche Quadrant." If he does say something negative you have to challenge him. In the most egregious cases you could do that publicly during the Q&A. Just write a note on the card provided and hand it in to the proctor. The moderator may not read it aloud but the analyst will see it. Analysts keep all the questions submitted at Gartner conferences as possible topics for future research notes. Don't insult him of course, but challenge his assumptions, support your case. He is keyed up and in tune at this moment. Your message will get through. Or follow up later with an email or a private conversation in the hall. But it is unlikely that he will slam you in public. If he truly has negative feelings about you he will just not mention you at all.

Assuming that all goes well, make sure to jot down some notes on what he said and follow up with a complimentary note later or if you bump into him later at the conference ask him some questions about what he said. Demonstrate that not only were you there, but you were listening.

The booth

Gartner events include a vendor expo area. The booths are usually a standard 10X10 feet or several of those combined. Gartner provides the booth and the usual expo amenities. You bring the signage, products, literature, and tchotchkes. You must have your booth manned by the sales team. The expo is the most target-rich environment they will ever be in. This is not a book on how to sell, but I have seen global VPs of sales completely fail at booth duty. They hide at the back of the booth, schmooze the CEO when she shows up and shoot the breeze with the other sales people. This is inexcusable. Send them to remedial sales training before the event if you have to. Even if they make no sales, if they talk to 100 CIOs in a day, one of those CIOs is bound to ask the analyst what he thinks about your products. That is a success along your path to execute on your MQ Plan. The sales people should be aware of who is attending and they should have made appointments with key prospects on their targeted list (please don't tell me they don't have such a list). They should be busy. Watch them. They will have no end of excuses for not being in the booth. If you are the CEO or VP of sales now is your chance to demonstrate leadership. Show the sales team how it is done. And most importantly, the entire booth team has to ensure that there is a buzz of activity in your booth for that important moment when the analyst passes by.

Keep an eye out for the analysts. Most of them feel (or are told by management) that it is their duty to breeze through the expo at least once. Some of them are unabashed tchotchke collectors. They will have big bags already full of plush toys, notebooks, pens, flashing shot glasses, and USB thumb drives. Don't disappoint them. Have something worthwhile for them to grab. At one Gartner show I saw a vendor give away an iPod to every single attendee that came to their booth. They had a line of prospects that wrapped halfway around the show floor. Not necessarily the best use of their money, but they certainly captured a lot of contacts.

So the analyst walks by. Grab her. Pull her into your booth. Take a picture of her standing with your CEO. And, most importantly, reinforce that seed you have planted in her brain. "Look Allison. See how our product fits in the kangaroo's pouch without disturbing her baby? Do you want to hold him?"

Dinner

If a Gartner sales person thinks she has a prospect on the line or if she has a big vendor client coming up for renewal she will schedule a dinner at a local restaurant with the client and one or more analysts. You might not be such a "whale," but if you are investing a significant amount in sponsorships and booth space you should try to negotiate a dinner with the analyst. Make sure your CEO is there. It's another chance to demonstrate to her that she is deriving value from all the money being spent. Treat the dinner as a social and bond-building event. Talk up your company of course, but not in a pitch. Instead of saying "we opened an office in the Netherlands" say "I had the most wonderful experience seeing the canals in Amsterdam on my last trip to our new office." You get the idea.

Breakfast

Gartner schedules "Breakfast with the Analyst" at these events. It is an opportunity for the attendees to rub shoulders with the great man (or woman). They are very awkward events for the analyst. He sits at a table with a placard with his name on it. As the table fills up, everyone sits as far from him as they can get. These are IT geeks, remember. They do fine at the evening events where drinks are flowing freely, but an early morning session where they are sitting at the same table with the guy they saw present to a standing-room-only audience the day before is a conversation killer. The best thing you can do is waltz in, sit right next to the analyst and strike up a conversation. Send your best morning person to do this. Talk about anything. Break the ice with the latest news report. Act as social secretary. Introduce yourself to everyone. Ask their names. If you know them, introduce them to the analyst. Ask the analyst questions that elicit stories. Most analysts are great story tellers. Get them going. Try to get the table engaged and the conversation flowing. You are doing the analyst a huge favor. Throughout the rest of the conference he will recognize these breakfast companions and perhaps have more productive conversations with them. Meanwhile ,you will be continuing your bond building.

Hospitality Suites

At most Gartner events vendors sponsor a hospitality suite, an empty room decked out for a party, and there is an evening of room-hopping between each party. The vendors vie for coolest party. There are Vegas-themed rooms with table games, there are ice-bars, there will probably be one with scantily clad women (please do not ever hire booth babes to represent your company. I don't care what your testosterone-soaked sales guys think. It is crass and misogynistic.) There is one vendor who attends the Gartner Security Summit every year and raffles off a fully decked-out Harley Davidson motorcycle. I have advised them that it is time to drop this extravagant gesture. There are better ways to spend your scant marketing resources. The analysts are obligated to visit all the hospitality suites, so track them down and schmooze them. Don't hound them of course, just contribute to their evening. And don't forget to reinforce your inception point: "Want to participate in our raffle? Just put your card in this wallaby's pouch!"

To sum up the Summit activity: just work it. Do as much as you can with the budget you have. The inception point might occur at the Summit in a casual conversation, at the booth, or late at night, when the analyst sits bolt up right in bed and exclaims: "Hey, those guys use marsupial pouches!"

CHAPTER THIRTEEN
Symposium

Gartner's IT Symposium and Expo is one of the biggest IT industry events of the year. Close to ten thousand IT professionals attend this extravaganza every fall at the Swan and Dolphin hotel complex at Disney World in Orlando, Florida. The event starts with registration and tutorial session on a Sunday and runs all the way through Friday. Its location lends itself to many dinners and events on the Disney World Boardwalk and beyond. Many Gartner analysts feel like Disney World is their second home--they have been there that often. This is the Big Show for analysts. Not all of them get asked to present, although you can expect a couple of hundred to be there. It is an amazing example of coordination and execution on the part of the Gartner staff and the Disney World conference crew. Imagine 10,000 people sitting down to buffet breakfast and lunch every day. They stream into gigantic tents and are quickly fed and pushed on their way to the opening Keynote each morning, where an industry giant will appear on stage with a senior Gartner analyst to be be grilled on the future of their industry. Michael Dell, Steve Balmer, John Thomson, Larry Ellison, and Steve Jobs have all been on that stage. From the keynotes, the attendees disperse to attend breakout sessions presented by Gartner analysts. They usually team up with one presenting and the other doing introductions and managing Q&A. Sometimes they prepare elaborate skits and live demos.

The value is tremendous for attendees, even at the breath-catching $3,895 ticket prices, not to mention travel, hotel, and time off from work. The attendees take it very seriously. They are there to learn. I met one who said it was his job to gather as much material as he could and regurgitate it for the IT team back at his place of work. CIOs, directors, and hands-on practitioners attend from all over the world. This is *the* event.

And you should attend. The costs are much higher than the smaller Gartner events, but the exposure is higher, also. If you sell to large enterprises and you have a sell-high strategy, this is where you are going to touch a large portion of your addressable market.

But it is not a focused conference. It pretty much covers the entire IT space. Maybe printers and fax machines are not covered, but most topics are, so the bigger vendors tend to populate the Expo. The high barrier to entry (in terms of fees) means that many of your competitors may not be there. Their marketing departments will have the same challenge you have convincing the CEO and CFO that you have to spend the money. And once you start attending, you have to keep it up. The analysts will pick up on the fact that you have pulled out.

So you have to make it pay. Even though sales has a big responsibility, it is up to marketing to track the leads and deals that get ignited by attending Symposium. Sales won't give anyone credit. They had already called on that client and it took a year after Symposium to close them, a year of meetings, deal making, and golfing. Still, the impact is there.

Most of the same opportunities to influence the analysts are available at Symposium as at a Summit, one-on-ones, breakfasts, dinners, etc., but keep in mind that the analysts are even busier than at the Summit.

For attendees, the high point of the week is Tuesday night. Gartner leases an entire Disney theme park for the evening. One hundred full-size buses ferry the attendees to the park where they are fed at dozens of food stations of every description, and they get free rides all night with no lines. The analysts are bound to be there, but they are there to have fun too. Even so, it does not hurt to take a ride on Space Mountain with your Gartner analyst. You may even get a chance to sit down with him or her and have a drink and food.

CHAPTER FOURTEEN
The CEO's Role

Of course the CEO cannot play a role unless she buys into the entire MQ plan. So that is the first step. Get buy-in. Couch the plan in terms of overall company goals. If the grand plan is to move into Michigan next year you cannot target the Leaders quadrant anytime soon. If the plan is to IPO at a $500 million valuation then the MQ plan better be to target the Leaders quadrant before the IPO (be cognizant of the quiet period. You won't be talking to analysts much leading up to the IPO, but that is alright. A successful IPO is just about the best thing you can do to boost that ability to execute metric). Assuming the CEO buys in to the plan, she also has to buy into her role. If she is not the technical lead for the company then she does not have to be the primary bond builder. Use this chapter to groom the CTO or technical founder for this.

There is also the evangelist role. Many vendors hire a big name to represent the company's vision to the press, analyst, and user communities. That is fine. Often it is a former analyst who has been given the title of Chief Strategy Officer. I have seen this work, although analysts do not make the best marketers.

Assuming that the CEO is tasked with the high-level bond building, here are her opportunities to influence the analyst.

Introductory briefing

A first Gartner briefing is a great opportunity for the CEO to introduce the company. The AR point of contact and the product expert should be on the call as well. The CEO delivers the message, the product expert the excitement.

Quarterly briefings

When it comes time to update the analyst on company progress the CEO is the best person to do this. Once again the product expert should be on the call to do the product update.

CEO = ability to execute
product expert = completeness of vision.

Drop by briefings

We already talked about this. The CEO is best positioned to do the drop-by briefing. And most likely to get the appointment.

Host of SAS days

Ideally, the CEO should be present for the entire SAS day as well as the dinner the night before. This is her baby after all. She should be interested enough to see it through. If she has to step out it should be for a reason that enhances the company image. "I'll be right back, we have a deployment problem in France and I have to make sure the team has landed and made it to the customer site. We had to get the Concorde out of mothballs to get them there today."

Gartner video production

Gartner has a pre-packaged video offering, Gartner Custom Multimedia Productions. The analyst provides context around the problem on camera and the company spokesperson (the CEO) talks about how they solve the problem. You can either go with Gartner's package or do the production yourself. Either way is expensive but once you have that video, market it everywhere. You are putting the analyst's face out there. He will watch it at least once and be exposed to the CEO's message one more time.

Road shows

For some reason road shows have fallen out of favor in recent years, probably because sales derides them as unproductive. They want marketing to produce easy-to-close leads for them, not to impose a visit to their territory by the CEO. The ten-city road show is one of the most effective ways to create a bond between the CEO and the analyst. Think about it. For at least twenty days out of the year the analyst is thinking about your company. They think about you as they brush up their presentation, as they head to the airport, before they go to sleep at the hotel in the evening, and most of the next day as they sit through the road-show seminar.

Here is the formula for a successful seminar. Believe me, I have done a lot of these.

The Gartner analyst goes first. He is why the attendees are there. Well, they want to hear the company pitch from the CEO, too, but you have marketed this event around the analyst. The analyst gives his standard pitch with perhaps some modifications based on the audience.

Then the analyst Q&A. Analysts are always comfortable doing Q&A.

The CEO presents the corporate pitch. Remember, the analyst is sitting there. He is going to hear this pitch ten times over the next few weeks. What a great opportunity to hammer home your message. Don't forget the inception point. By the tenth seminar the analyst will be talking about how important it is to include pouches in your marsupial tracking strategy.

And then the winning element of a successful seminar. A satisfied customer, ideally one from the local community, presents on: 1. The problem he was having 2. How he chose you 3. How you solved his problem and life is good.

Now close the event, give everyone their package of goodies, and rush the analyst off to lunch with a key customer in that city. After lunch let the analyst go so he can catch up on email and get to the airport.

There is one more important element of a successful event and that is that the room should be packed. That is sales' job, so we will address that in the next chapter.

Host of webinars

It is also valuable to get the CEO to host any webinars you do with an analyst. She can do the introductions and pass it off to the analyst who presents on the issue and the market, then the product expert presents on the solution. Save time for Q&A at the end. Aside from keeping your attendees on the call you will keep the analyst engaged. You can only hope he is listening to the product pitch one more time. If you don't do Q&A it is guaranteed you will lose the analyst's attention. He will be answering email until it comes time to sign off.

Direct calls

Once a bond of sorts is created between the analyst

and the CEO it will be possible for the CEO to call the analyst directly. Don't abuse this earned privilege. Call with a quick question, even if it is to ask about that restaurant in Cancun the analyst mentioned because he has a meeting with the President of Mexico to talk about marsupials. If the analyst does not pick up (they rarely do), leave a cogent message and tell him you will drop him an email, no need to call back. One of the purposes of infrequent calls is you want to keep the channel of communication open. Someday the analyst will have a question. If he has the CEO's phone number in his contacts he will call. If he has to go through the AR person, he may not.

Gartner sales person

I do not know if this has ever happened, but I think it would be a brilliant tactic. In the next chapter we talk about the role of sales in getting customer CIOs to talk to Gartner. But this tactic turns that around. The CEO can play a roll in getting customers to become Gartner clients. If you have a happy customer who happens to be a large enterprise, encourage him to become a Gartner client. Become a salesperson for Gartner. Pitch the value of the inquiry: how you can get quick access to an industry expert to answer major product selection questions. Talk up the value of Gartner events. If you succeed, the Gartner salesperson is going to be grateful, which can pay dividends when negotiating your own Gartner engagement. And, you have salted the mine just slightly in your favor. Give it a try. Be sure to let me know how it works.

CHAPTER FIFTEEN
The Role of the Sales Team

The sales team can be your biggest liability in trying to achieve positive movement in your quest to move UP and to the RIGHT. Look at all the ways they interfere:

1. They are over-promising to clients. They make a sale and drop the client like a rabid kangaroo (had enough of my marsupial references yet?). This leaves your over-taxed support staff and engineering to pick up the slack. Sure they are increasing sales but they are probably generating disgruntled calls to Gartner about how to address an unresponsive help desk.

2. Without your knowledge, they trap the analyst in a hospitality suite or bar and give them a piece of their mind about how they should be the Leader.

3. They disrupt your carefully planned strategy to update your Wikipedia entry by posting all sorts of positive statements that get thrown out by the editors and increase the vigilance the editors expend on your entry.

4. They undermine your efforts with the CEO by complaining bitterly that marketing is not doing its job because the analysts aren't saying great things about you or moving the dot fast enough.

It goes on. If you are in marketing, you know the issues. More vendors are sales driven than marketing driven. The sales VP is the second most important person at the executive staff meetings. He is the one that drives the company forward and provides the profits that fuel growth. Marketing is a cost center.

Get the VP of sales to buy into the MQ plan, too. The CEO should help with this. The MQ plan is the responsibility of the entire organization (I am practicing what I preach: repetition). Give the sales team a copy of this book. They are going to love this chapter.

There are three things the sales team has to do to push the MQ plan forward.

1. Do no harm. Never confront the analyst. Not in comments on their blogs, not on Twitter, not on LinkedIn. Do not denigrate the MQ. Most sales people are coached in objection handling. It's part of Sales 101. When they encounter the objection that the prospect's CIO only invites Magic Quadrant Leaders to bid, the natural tendency is to tear down Gartner and its short sighted analysts. Give them material from Gartner that can support their efforts. Educate them. Someday you are going to be in that Leaders Quadrant and the sales team is going to reap the

biggest benefit.

2. Populate the road show with attendees. Most sales people, for all their vaunted rolodexes, are horrible at this. When I was at Gartner, I saw this repeatedly. A big vendor contracted with Gartner for six lunch seminars in major cities around the US. The meeting rooms were in nice hotels, and set up for 40 attendees. No more than six showed up at any event. I took it personally. I thought it meant no one wanted to hear what I had to say. It did not really hurt my impression of the vendor, just my impression of their ability to market. It was only in later years that I realized that it is sales' responsibility to put butts in seats. Marketing puts together the roadshow, they purchase a mailing list and they send out 50,000 emails. But that is a single touch, at most two if they send out a reminder.

When I re-launched IT-Harvest in September of 2008 I foolishly committed to filling two dinner events with director-level IT buyers in New York City. It was a lot of work. I reached out to my own contact list. My fans. I got a dozen commitments for each event and the vendor filled the rest of the seats with the help of their local sales team. The dinners were scheduled for the week that Lehman Brothers collapsed. The Lehman folks had trouble explaining to their spouses why they were going to a fancy dinner at the 21 Club when they had just lost their jobs. They were no-shows. We still pulled the event off, but it gave me first-hand appreciation for how hard it is to fill seats. I have a lot more luck in Australia, where they do not get as much attention from analysts. I'll still commit to filling seats but I charge a lot more!

Every successful seminar series I have participated in, the local sales team has done the heavy lifting. They blast their contacts with personal invitations to the event. They call them up. They beat the bushes. And they re-call everyone who has signed up the night before, to guilt them into honoring their commitment. "Man my CEO is going to be there. If you don't show it will look like I am ineffective! And bring your buddy from the bowling team, too."

Even though the sales team may not want to support the booth at the Gartner events, they still have to participate. There is nothing so telling to an analyst as seeing your booth empty at a crowded show. The sales team is responsible for building that buzz on the show floor. Help them find out who is attending so they can invite their contacts and prospects to drop by the booth and meet the CEO and sales engineers in person.

CHAPTER SIXTEEN
Managing Wikipedia

Before we delve into the tips and tricks of social media let us pause for a moment to consider your Wikipedia entry. After your corporate website, the entry in Wikipedia for your organization is arguably the most important public-facing web property that tells the world who you are and what you do. There is just one problem you do not own it and you may not have even been involved in the creation of the content. If you try to edit it in your favor the, it could backfire.

Not every analyst will think to check the Wikipedia entries on the vendors they track, but the good ones do. On top of that, journalists, bloggers, potential investors, and new hires will be looking at your entry. Of course you want it to display your company and products in the best light.

Many organizations have changed or attempted to change their Wikipedia entries. Often they bungle the job. A tool called Wikiscanner has even been developed to identify the source of such changes. *The New York Times* reported:

"(In 2006) someone at PepsiCo deleted several paragraphs of the Pepsi entry that focused on its detrimental health effects. In 2005, someone using a computer at Diebold deleted paragraphs that criticized the company's electronic voting machines. That same year, someone inside Wal-Mart Stores changed an entry about employee compensation."

You have to take control of your Wikipedia page, and you have to do it subtly. Let us use the example of one company as a case in point. When I joined this company as CMO, its Wikipedia entry was a disaster. This global network security appliance vendor had an entry that included only the following:

"The company had been engaged in a controversy over its violations of GPL licensing for the way they used the Linux operating system in their products.

"The company's products were purchased by the government of Myanmar, a military dictatorship, and restricted by the US State Department."

The Wikipedia entry classified the company as a vendor of censorware. Not good, you will agree.

On top of this nightmare every new employee, especially sales hires, would go in and update the Wikipedia entry with a bunch of flowery language laced with marketing speak (best, leading, acclaimed, etc.). The ever-vigilant Wikipedia editors, who are all volunteers, and many are rabidly protective of the entries they monitor, would flag the updates and reject them. The editors are on the lookout for this type of flagrant abuse and over-vigilant in preventing it.

I gave responsibility for fixing this problem to our Analyst Relations person who also happened to be the savviest person in the marketing department when it came to the web and social networking. There are many lessons to be learned from her successful resolution of a major marketing issue.

First she created a new account on Wikipedia, one not associated with her employment. Because Wikipedia tracks the IP address from which updates are posted, she made sure to only make edits from home or remote work spaces. Then, over a period of several months she slowly added new information. She did not remove the embarrassing (although true) items that were there--she just buried them under real information. She kept her updates devoid of marketing-speak and stuck to the facts. Every entry she made was supported with a citation from an independent third party. Yahoo! press releases do not cut it; only news articles or factual web resources that aren't considered "partners" of the company.

By studying the intricacies of Wikipedia entries, she learned to create a side bar that listed key executives, key dates, location of offices, and financials. That part was easy, she reports.

Updating the body was harder. She created a table of contents that was logically structured with sections for Business, Finances, and Products, and, incidentally, moved the offending reports from a subheading of "Controversy" to one labeled "Other" at the very bottom of the Wikipedia entry. The newer content was voluminous enough to push that section below the first screen, but it kept true to Wikipedia's stringent guidelines.

This was a painstaking process. And just when she had accomplished her goal, and the Wikipedia entry fixed, an overzealous employee torpedoed her efforts by doing his own updates – despite requests for no one to touch the page. Wikipedia was on to him immediately, and reverted the site all the way back to the original entry. She had to start over.

So, lessons learned:

-Craft a strategy. Plan for 6-12 months
-Assign one person to be the wiki-shepherd
-Alert the entire organization to keep their well-intentioned paws off
-Meticulously add the content you want, never removing the original content
-Provide citations to every single statement made
-Monitor the site continuously, especially during PR crises, when spurious updates are most likely to occur and when journalists are most likely to visit.
-Don't be afraid of Wikipedia. Ongoing factual updates (financials, leadership, etc.) are acceptable. Just steer clear of spinning the story.

If there is an error, the best procedure is to log into Wikipedia and go to the "talk" section on your entry. Identify yourself with your employer and politely point out any discrepancies or errors. Provide links to data and third parties that support your position.

One admonishment. Never update your competitors' Wikipedia entries. Some overzealous Congressional aides have been caught at this. It's bad form and probably illegal although I know of no cases in the vendor world.

By following this strategy and using the techniques described above you will have ensured that your organization is shown in the best possible light.

CHAPTER SEVENTEEN
Leveraging Social Media

There are plenty of books on social media, including specialized books on Twitter, LinkedIn, and even one by Guy Kawasaki on Google+. See the appendix for a list of resources. But I have some ideas on how to leverage social media for influence, in particular analyst influence. This chapter is a complete revelation, for the first time, of the things I have learned about social media and analyst influence. I have had a little more time to investigate and use social media than most analysts, other than the ones that cover social media, that is. Here are my techniques, tips, and gems.

Twitter

Twitter is a powerful influence tool if used properly. One of the reasons it is so valuable is that journalists and PR people jumped on early. Social media marketing is the latest thing in their field and they are all over it. Journalists and PR people are critical components of the influence eco-system.

Luckily, they are all on Twitter.

Let's quickly go over what Twitter is. It is broadcast instant messaging with extremely low barriers to following people. When it first started out, the idea behind Twitter was that instead of texting your friends individually about the meet-up at the local bar, you could send one message and have it sent to everyone who elected to follow your "tweets" straight to their phones. Obviously that did not scale. Imagine getting a text message for every tweet in your stream today!

Now Twitter is a medium for posting short messages, news items, links to interesting stories or the latest meme, and yes, what you are doing at the moment. There are over 140 million active users of Twitter.

If you are not already on Twitter, it is almost impossible to understand the value. So go to Twitter.com and sign up today. You will soon reap the rewards.

Create an account. As with all social media the early adopters grab all the great IDs. You will need Twitter accounts for:

Your company

If you are lucky this will be available. If your name is trademarked you should be able to wrest control from whomever grabbed it. If a Twitter squatter is sitting on it, this should be fairly straightforward. If you are the Weather Company or the Smith Company it will be much harder to get @weather or @smith. (That is how you address a Tweet to someone; you "at" them by putting the @ sign in front of their ID). You can go with appending "TheOfficial" to your name.

Your CEO

If your CEO is already active on Twitter you are off to a great start. If not, get her the Twitter ID @YourCompanyCEO.

Your social media influence expert

This is the person you are going to assign to manage all of your social media activity. She or he will ideally already be a very active Twitter user.

Every employee in your company

That's right, every single employee and stake holder has a role to play in social media.

Next, build your Twitter page. Fill out the the profile for each of the above roles. The company and a link to your homepage should appear in the profile summary that everyone sees. Always use a professional picture of the account holder if it is a person, and the company logo or an image that represents the company for the company ID.

You also have the ability to upload a background image. Have your graphics people come up with a great corporate background that includes an image that depicts what you do. If it evokes the inception point, even better.

Now you are all set. There is just one problem. There are four little numbers that appear on your page: the number of times you have tweeted, the number of people you follow, the number of people who follow you, and the number of lists you appear on. You must grow all of those stats as quickly as possible.

If you treat Twitter like Facebook you will fail. You want everyone to follow you, and you want to follow everyone. The only IDs you don't want are spammers. We all have to do our part to weed out spammers.

The secret to getting followers

The number of followers you have is loosely associated with your influence. The most followed people are celebrities, journalists, and the early social media experts. When they Tweet something people pay attention. It's the Oprah effect. If Justin Bieber tweets that he likes Coke more than Pepsi, buy stock in Coke and sell Pepsi short. The rest of us are not that popular. The typical industry analyst will have one or two thousand followers, as you saw during your influence measurement exercise.

So, the goal is to get as many followers as possible as quickly as you can. Here is how you do that:

Follow followers. Thanks to the limits that Twitter

imposes this rule is the key to getting followers. Twitter will only let you follow 2,000 people until you get to around 1,800 followers. Twitter also limits how many people you can follow in a day. The number is fluid but you will hit it during your growth phase. Once you get past 1,800 followers you can start following like mad, but there are still limits to curtail abuse. So let's continue to see how to abuse Twitter.

You do not want to follow Justin Bieber, CNN Breaking News, or any of the other interesting accounts. Those accounts do not follow you back. You can look at any Twitter account to see the ratio of followed to followers. It is really apparent who follows back and who does not. If they have 10,000 followers and only follow 134 people they will not follow you back unless they know you.

Let's get started. You are going to find and follow people who follow back. Go to www.twitter.com/stiennon and follow me. I will follow you back. There's one. Now click on my followers and follow the first twenty that are listed. Don't follow the people I follow, you don't know that they follow back. But the people who follow me have already self-identified as followers. And you only follow the first twenty because they have been recently active. Someone who followed me six months ago might not even use Twitter anymore.

Now go to the Twitter page of someone you just followed and click on the list of *their* followers. Follow the first twenty in that list. Rinse and repeat until

Twitter says you have followed too many people. Do this for each account you manage.

The next day, after the Twitter clock has been reset, start over. Follow the limit.

If you follow people randomly, you get about 10% follow backs. If you use the technique above it is closer to 50%. Here is how you get that number closer to 90%.

There is a search bar on your Twitter page. Search on "#followback" or "#Teamfollowback". You will get a list of people engaged in building their Twitter follower numbers. Ninety percent of them will follow back.

By this point you are going to hit the Follow wall. Twitter will stop you from following any more people until the number of followers you have catches up. So, you must un-follow the losers who did not follow you back.

Go to justunfollow.com_and login with your Twitter ID. Un-follow everyone who has not followed you. There are dozens of tools for doing this. I find the free ones are good, but if you are serious pay the small fee that allows you to unfollow more people efficiently.

Now you have to take protective measures to ensure that people who followed you do not think you are a loser who does not follow back. Just look at your list of followers and follow all of them. It's only polite, and you spent about three seconds getting every follower, you don't want to throw *that* away.

Eventually you will want to use an auto-followback tool to take care of this task.

TwitterGrader and Klout pay attention to the your follow/follower ratio. Rightly so, as a true influencer will have many more followers than follows. So, keep your ratio in favor of followers by eliminating people who do not follow back. If you need to up your Klout score you can always un-follow everyone and get an instant boost, but I have not encountered a reason to do that.

As you will see, this process does not really advance your cause. Once you get over 2,000 followers you can start to cultivate real people that are of interest to you. Follow every journalist, analyst, and blogger in your space. You can skip most of the TV news anchors, they don't do much journalism, as you know. Also follow PR people and the people they follow.

Follow everyone in your company and make sure they follow back the corporate accounts. You are going to monitor their tweets and leverage their activity.

Now to work. Every day of the year you are going to continue getting new followers, but you are also going to start to engage the analysts.

It is important to realize that most people do not actually read their Twitter stream, that constant flow of tweets from people they follow. They can't. Most people only log in to Twitter when they have something to post. After posting a link to their latest blog post, or a news item that piqued their interest, they then check the "Mentions" button marked with an @ sign. This will show all of the tweets that are either directed at them, a response to something they tweeted usually, or anyone at all on Twitter that mentioned them--even people they do not follow. In this way they can engage in conversations publicly or respond to comments made about them. Many people will also search on their name which could be different from their Twitter ID.

This is how you get noticed by the analysts, journalists, and bloggers, even if they do not follow you. You can @ anyone who does not block you. So proceed to:

-Re-tweet influencers. Don't go crazy, but once a week, at least, re-tweet something interesting or appropriate they say. If they tweet a link to their latest blog or article or upcoming webinar, re-tweet that. Help them out. Drive traffic and followers their way.

-Mention them. If an influencer is mentioned in the press, wins an award, or takes on a new role, tweet that. Either use their name or @ them.

-If you meet an influencer, tweet about that.

-If a journalist tweets that she is looking for a source, tweet back and suggest the analyst.

-#FF the influencers. #FF is the hash tag for Follow Friday. I have no idea who invented this, but it has become a Twitter tradition every Friday to tweet lists of great people to follow, preceded by #FF. Your tweet might be "#FF Great marsupial tracking analysts @analyst1, @analyst2."

All of the above activity is bound to get you noticed by the influencers. They may even have followed you back by now. To get them to follow you, make sure there is some real value in doing so. The corporate TwitterID at least should be posting everything about the company. If the analyst stubbornly refuses to follow back send a Tweet like this: "@analyst1 Hey Allison, follow me back so I can DM you."

A DM is Twitter's way of facilitating private conversations: Direct Messages. If an analyst is following you, you will see a little mail icon when you visit her Twitter page. Click on that and you can send her a message. Use an upcoming briefing, an opportunity to talk to a journalist, or any other excuse to engage her in conversation. Keep the activity going. Every touch moves you along in your MQ plan.

Now enlist the rest of the company. Encourage employees as well as stakeholders, like investors and board members, even channel partners, to get on the Twitter wagon. Email them weekly alerts with suggestions of things to Tweet. Advise them to follow the corporate account and re-tweet important messages. Find your Twitter users that already have a lot of followers and ask them to also re-tweet company news.

LinkedIn

LinkedIn has some of the same value as Twitter. It

has its own strengths too.

Make sure your profile and that of all the key executives are up to date and polished. There should be professional images of each profile owner. Ensure that the description of their responsibilities at their current employer (your company) is accurate and reflects the great things that are happening there. Don't use the same words in each profile or it will look like blatant marketing. It *is* marketing, but it should be skillful marketing.

Encourage every employee to sign up for LinkedIn. This can be dangerous because headhunters and competitors are sharks in the water and activity on a LinkedIn profile is like chum to them. It *is* true that when people are thinking about moving on they start to polish their profile. But that is not a problem at your company, you are thriving and no one would want to leave, right?

If they are truly keeping an eye on the space they cover, an analyst will be monitoring LinkedIn for signs of a mass exodus or rapid growth in employees. If you have a lot of employees, you are going to give the impression that you are growing quickly if you get them all to sign up for LinkedIn.

After your first meeting with an analyst, or anyone in the Influence Pyramid, request a connection on LinkedIn. Most people use LinkedIn as a rolodex. The analysts should not be too snobby about accepting LinkedIn requests.

Consider placing ads on LinkedIn.

Connect to the analysts' influencers. If you know who the analyst respects--other analysts, journalists, authors, speakers--reach out to them via LinkedIn. Make a connection and nurture a relationship.

FaceBook

FaceBook is an enigma for marketers. The numbers of people on FaceBook is attractive, but for the most part people use FaceBook to interact with friends and family. Inserting a professional relationship is often difficult. One technique that is beginning to work is to create a FaceBook page for the company and request analysts and other influencers to "Like" it. Unless they opt out they will then get a notice every time you post to the page and they may even see it in their News Feed. Don't abuse this with too many pictures of staff having fun at your events. Post events, webinars, major news, and alerts about things that impact your industry. Certainly post news of favorable coverage in the press.

Google+

Google+ is Google's answer to FaceBook. It is remarkably similar in its features. At this writing Google+ has failed to catch on as a good social networking tool for marketers. That said, make sure that all of your content is given a +1 by you and your team. There may be some advantage for SEO and if an influencer is in the "circle" of anyone who gives it a +1 they may see the content. It can't hurt.

Like Twitter you can add influencer's to your "circles" (similar to following on Twitter) without their buy-in. They will see that you added them but do not have to add you to a circle in return. It is a subtle touch point that may pay dividends so go ahead and "circle" all of your influencers.

Blogging

Every vendor should maintain one or more blogs. At the very least you should maintain a technical blog written by your CTO or members of your research team. The content should contribute to the body of knowledge in your space. You probably employee some of the experts in the field, possibly *the* expert. Break news in your blog and point tech journalists to it. They may not link directly to your blog but they will quote it and the author.

Many vendors also maintain blogs written by their CEOs. These can be powerful tools of influence. Journalists, customers, and even analysts are likely to read them, especially if the content is heartfelt and obviously written by the CEO and not the marketing staff.

You can hire guest bloggers too. If they are influencers in their own right they will draw an audience and their message will be heard.

Many sites such as Forbes.com and ZDNet.com are open to industry experts that have recurring good content. These sites get indexed by Google News so anyone who as an alert set up on relevant key words will see when you post. Posts to these sites can go viral and garner tens of thousands of views. If you can convince the editors of these sites that your content will not be self-serving and overtly commercial they will welcome the increased traffic you bring them.

A recent trend is for vendors to attempt to set up independent blogs that are not directly associated with their company or products. This can be very effective, especially when you are trying to generate more interest in your product category and the problems you address. If there is no site like this today in your space you may consider the investment. It requires professional editors and writers and full time web staff. Creating a valuable source of unbiased information on an emerging space can an effective way to increase coverage.

Leveraging social media for influence is a new discipline. Treat it like an experiment. Try new things every day. Figure out what works. Rinse and repeat.

CHAPTER EIGHTEEN
Guerrilla Tactics

I have saved the best for almost last: Guerrilla tactics for analyst influence. Fit these into the rest of your MQ plan when they are called for or as the opportunity presents itself. Most are derived from what I have seen work either on me as an analyst or by vendors I have known who managed to perhaps rise higher than they belonged in an otherwise objective Magic Quadrant. Being out of place--too far UP and to the RIGHT- is a tenuous position.

As mentioned in the Influence Pyramid; the people who have the most influence on a Gartner analyst are their customers. Gartner's strength, and frankly industry dominance, comes from its client base that cuts across the Global 10,000. It is the analysts' daily engagement with IT professionals that gives them insight into trending topics and vendor momentum. Analyst's use trends they observe to determine topics for new Research Notes (RNs). If there are a flood of inquiries on a topic that has not been covered before, the analyst will write a note on it. The RN is published and the inquiry desk starts sending it out in response to client questions. The hope is to limit the number of times the analyst has to answer the same question. Invariably, this backfires. Publishing a note is like lighting a beacon. It announces that the analyst has something to say on the subject and it generates even more calls as clients home in on the beacon.

How many calls on the same subject alert an analyst to a hot topic? You will be surprised. Three. Yes, three calls on the same topic in a short time frame, say two weeks, is a major indicator. They may only take 20 calls in those two weeks. If three of them are on the same topic that is 15% of all calls! An analyst may check with the other analysts in the group. If they are fielding calls on the same thing, a Major Trend is underway.

You can see where I am going with this. If you could increase the number of calls about your product you could shine that beacon on your company. But how? It is not easy. I have tried. I have identified the method but have only seen it put into play a couple of times.

You must determine who among your customer base are Gartner clients. The only way to do that is to ask them. and the only people that can do that are your sales people. Oh no! Not only that, but the sales people have to ask those clients to please make Gartner inquiries about your products. A sales person is going to be very leery of doing that. What if the analyst kills the deal he is working on? This is a very real, but not great risk.

An analyst can track the progress of a deal. The first call from the client will be to ask who should be on their short list. The analyst invariably walks them through the Magic Quadrant. For the most part, he will support any company that the client has already chosen to put on their short list and is in the Leaders Quadrant. If the vendor is an "IBM house", he will support IBM which is probably in the Challenger Quadrant because he knows the internal resistance the buyer will get if they go against the grain. If the client is looking at Visionaries he will question why. If they are looking at Niche players he will raise objections. Rarely will he tell a client that picking any vendor on the MQ is a mistake.

The next call from the client, sometimes six months later, will be to report on the results of a bake-off or a proof-of-concept and the questions will be about purchasing. The analyst will provide advice on price, support contracts, and other items to watch out for that they have learned from clients who have purchased from the same vendor.

As you can see, there are multiple opportunities to get noticed by the analyst. If only you could encourage more of your customers to make inquiries. It does not take many. If the analyst starts to see that you are displacing incumbents and beating out competitors, your reputation will soar.

I would like to say you could offer some incentive to your salesforce to add this new task to their list--

asking their prospects to call Gartner, I mean. But the only measurable incentive is the eventual boost to your standing in the eyes of the analyst and the subsequent movement UP and to the RIGHT in the Magic Quadrant. So explain the process to them at the next all-hands meeting or sales off-site. There is some minor risk to each sale, but the overall risk is low and the payback enormous. Pose it like this: Take the minor risk now, reap the rewards later when your product is in the Leaders Quadrant and included on *every* short list.

There is nothing underhanded in the foregoing. Unfortunately the reality is that you *are* selling to Gartner clients, but only a few ever call in. Perhaps it is because your product choice is a no-brainer. It does more, costs less, and is better supported. The client does not feel the need for guidance from Gartner.

This next tip *could* be underhanded so I am *not* recommending it. Let me just tell you about an incident that had tremendous impact on me. I was doing a road show for a particular vendor. Of course, I was not supporting that vendor's products. As always with Gartner analysts there is no taint of product preference in these paid speaking engagements. The vendor hopes that the Gartner blessing is going to be assumed by attendees, but Gartner survives based on their reputation for objectivity. After the event, a local IT guy came up to me. He was ecstatic about a product he had purchased and deployed. It was not the product of the vendor who had hosted the luncheon event. His statement was "this stuff is amazing, it just works!" I had never heard such an unsolicited accolade about *any* product in the space. His statement was completely heartfelt. While it had tremendous influence on me, I still wonder to this day if that end-user had been planted. Did a competing vendor somehow induce him to buttonhole me? Or was he truly enthusiastic, to the point of being a fan and wanting to spread the word? It happens. But it is extremely rare.

I will not suggest you send someone to your competitor's events to snow an analyst. I *will* suggest that you should create as many rabid fans of your product as possible. It will eventually get back to the analyst.

Targeted advertising

I am a big fan of traditional advertising. It is a multi-billion dollar business. It has been proven to work over and over. If it didn't work, why would commercial television still exist? How do you suppose beer gets sold anyway? So why don't IT vendors advertise? My theory is that many IT vendors are led by engineers who tried advertising once in the early days of their company or even at the first company they founded. Some slick salesman sold them on a magazine insert, or those television shows that supposedly run in airports and on airplanes that nobody ever sees. They shelled out $10K and never saw any results. They are still smarting from that bad experience and have vowed to never repeat it. And of course just about every CFO will support *that* decision. All the CFO sees is the expense this quarter. He never sees the increase in sales two quarters from now thanks to increased brand awareness and incoming calls. He thinks that is from increased investment in the sales force. Why is the bottom right-hand ad that appears on the front page of the Financial Times always for $10,000 watches? Why are there never ads for $10,000 switches, routers, or servers?

This is not the place to convince you that advertising is a good thing. But there is a special case of advertising that you can use to your advantage: ads that are laser targeted at the analyst. Ideally, every time your analyst opens the *Wall Street Journal* or the *New York Times,* she would see an ad for your product, one that reinforces your inception point. I guarantee you, analysts still read newspapers. So think about other ways you can get your ads in front of an analyst.

Before I tell you a story from the old-school ad days, a real "Mad Men" story, let me plant a suggestion. Say you were going to place an ad. Who is your target audience? The IT buyers right? Wrong. The analysts. Work with an ad agency to come up with several ad mock-ups. It's fun. Ad people are great to work with. They are energetic, creative, and excited about your products. You can get several firms to compete by presenting their ideas in mock-up form.

Then, schedule an inquiry with the analyst to review the mock-ups. Ask them what they think is the best ad. Then run *that* ad! How is that for targeting? When they see the ad they will like it. Game over.

OK, "Mad Men" story. Back in the day, an automotive parts supplier was positioning itself for the next model of Ford sedan. They planned on running ads on drive-time radio. This was the old days, remember. But automotive sales, especially back then, were a different animal. A parts supplier was engaged in a year-long effort to win the deal for, say, a new engine, or an instrument panel, or a suspension system. If they won the deal there was a 5-10 year development phase, huge capital investment to build a new plant down the road from the assembly plant, and then years of profit until the next complete redesign. So the parts supplier, who knew the identity of the purchasing agent who would make the final decision, deployed someone to monitor the parking lot outside the purchasing agent's office in Dearborn. When he parked his car and walked into work, this old-school operative strolled up to it, looked through the window and read what band his radio was tuned to! (I told you this was a long time ago). The parts supplier then ran its radio ads on that station during the decision maker's commute to work. Now *that* is targeted advertising.

How can you get creative and come up with ways to target an analyst with your ads? Here are a few of my ideas. Not all of them of course. The analysts read this book too!

Airport ads

Have your ad agency attempt to get display ads in your analyst's home airport. Analysts travel--a lot. They are going to be passing through their home airport at least twice a week. What if they saw your display ad that often? What if it was the very ad they had chosen? This may be over the top, but what if the ad was a *picture of the analyst* with a cogent side-bar quote? You would have to work with Gartner to accomplish that.

Expand your airport display ad program to the airports in tech-heavy areas like San Francisco, San Jose, Boston, New York, London, Frankfurt, and Chicago. If your major competitor is, say, IBM, buy display ads in the Westchester County airport. Your analyst will probably be flying in there at least once a year. What better time to remind him of your existence than when he is paying a visit to your competitor?

For that matter, lock up all the display ad space in the Westchester County Airport today. That airport is the closest to Gartner's headquarters in Stamford, Connecticut. I have passed through it many times on my way to the Gartner Briefing Center at headquarters. LaGuardia is the other airport that serves Stamford.

Regional ads

Many newspapers have separate print runs in major regions. This helps them to sell more targeted ads to those companies that do not need, or cannot afford, to blanket the US or the world with their message. Think about a display ad that covers the analyst's home region. You could even ask the analyst at some point in your briefings, inquiries, or conference interactions what papers she reads. Be subtle: "Did you see that article in today's print edition of the *Wall Street Journal*?" It would be creepy to stake out the analyst's house to see what paper is delivered in the morning.

Radio advertising

Per the "Mad Men" story above, you can do radio ads too. These are easily targeted at the analyst's location. Your local sales person will love the attention you are giving to his region. You may even find that his sales spike, a good indicator that advertising works. But how to find out what radio stations the analyst listens to? You can always ask. But it is going to be harder to make sure they hear it. I suspect that sponsoring the local NPR affiliate is your best bet. Analysts gravitate towards NPR thanks to the in-depth reporting and interviews with experts.

Billboards

This is another audacious tactic. Place billboard ads in the analyst's home town. If there is a prime placement along his route to the airport, grab it. While you are at it place a billboard near the airport where your company is headquartered. Anyone who flies in to see you will see your ad. The analyst coming to the SAS day might see it too.

Direct mail

Everyone knows that direct mail sucks. Response rates are measured in tenths of a percent. But you are not going to blast 100,000 addresses with your fliers and offers. You are going to send out a very targeted mailer to one address. That's right, send the analyst stuff. It will be such an unusual occurrence that the analyst *will* read it.

I can recall two direct mail campaigns that were effective. The first was a network appliance company, Netcontinuum, that sent a series of packages containing tools: a hammer, a screw driver, a coping saw, and finally a branded tool box to hold them. I still have the tool box even though the vendor is long gone, and I can remember the vendor's name to this day.

The other great mailing was one by Fortinet, the network security appliance vendor. They sent out 1,000 of the their small office firewalls to IT security directors, who invariably handed them to one of their tech guys who installed it at home. Years later, I would run into sales situations where the deal was won because the decision maker was familiar with the product because he still used it at home.

So go ahead and mail your coffee cup, your mouse pad, or some cleverly designed gimmick to the analyst. It can't hurt and it can enforce your brand and your message.

Online ads

Of course, the analyst is online all day. While online display ads are most effective for impulse buying, they do play a small role in branding through sheer repetition. Advertise a white paper the analyst will actually want to read. There are some techniques to attempt to target the analyst. Purchase Google Key Words for any company in the MQ, especially your own. If you have hired the analyst to present at a roadshow or online event, advertise that. Make sure the analyst's name is featured. This is a contributor to the next guerrilla technique.

Make the analyst famous

The analysts you work with are already famous in their own way. They command the instant respect that comes with the Gartner brand. But their career success depends on getting their name out there. Only by gaining industry recognition will they rise in esteem among their peers, and ultimately contribute to Gartner's brand and growth. If there is one analyst who happens to "get" your industry and has recognized what you are doing as important or effective, then the more you can contribute to her reputation and the more her thoughts will be listened to. Here are some effective techniques to enhance an analyst's brand:

Get the analyst quoted

Gartner tracks quotes internally and reports on them. If an analyst is quoted in mainstream media, he might show up on the front page of the Gartner internal website. Most vendors attempt to get a quote from the analyst for their press releases. That is fine, but even better is to have your PR team reach out to journalists and actively push the analyst for comments on stories the journalist is working on. Let the analyst know you have done this, even ask permission beforehand.

Adopt the analyst's terminology

Every analyst wants to identify the next category. It is a major milestone for an analyst when her term for an emerging market is adopted by industry. Help that process along. At the beginning of the development cycle, every vendor is also attempting to define the space with a term that positions them as the leader. "It's marsupial pouch tracking (MPT), not nocturnal creature intelligence (NCI)." It is the analyst's job to define an industry, not the vendor's. So go with what your analyst has chosen. Don't fight it, promote it. The one who invents the term is the expert, maybe even the "father of" the space.

Get the analyst promoted

Promote the analyst to Gartner management. Start with your Gartner sales rep. Summits and the IT Symposium are opportune moments to chat with Gartner executive management. Upper management may not even know the name of your analyst. Make sure they do. Of course you do not have to lay it on thick. You can even be negative. Analysts are judged by how much impact they have. Pissing off the vendors could be a good thing for the analyst. Negative comments from end-user clients are of course bad, so get your friends who are CIOs at major companies to drop the analyst's name often.

More guerrilla techniques

Get the analyst hired

Not happy with the Gartner analyst that covers your space? Create a new Gartner analyst who is predisposed to your way of thinking. Gartner is always looking for new talent. The qualifications are someone who is knowledgable in a space who can write, speak, and work hard. If there is a prolific blogger, podcaster, speaker in your space that you like, push them to consider joining Gartner. Use your contacts there to get him interviewed. Make introductions, write a recommendation.

This strategy can backfire of course. Many a president has appointed a Supreme Court Justice based on his belief that the judge will lean one way or the other on critical social issues, only to be disappointed. Uh oh. Did I just draw a comparison between Gartner analysts and Supreme Court Justices? I am taking this topic way too seriously.

Get the analyst fired

Don't even go there. This has never worked to my knowledge. My early career in automotive was during the great transition to supplier design and engineering. In the early '80s the auto companies began pushing the responsibility for their designs to the manufacturers, who stepped up by hiring engineers and managers to take on this new responsibility. But the auto company would still employ a program manager whose job was to oversee the entire development project and interface with the rest of the division working on the vehicle. Sometimes that program manager would be a pain in the ass. He would nit-pick, make changes, and even work actively to change suppliers. So the supplier would hire him away with a big salary and a corner office in hopes that the replacement program manager would be easier to work with. Then they would give the new executive hire inconsequential stuff to do in the hopes that he would quit out of boredom. I have not seen this tried in the tech industry, but there are plenty of cases of vendors hiring away the analyst who covers their space, usually into a strategy role. That is certainly one way to get the attention of the other Gartner analysts. It helps to have someone who knows the inner workings of Gartner on your team. Briefings can go really well if the new hire is well respected by the other analysts. But make sure you use that ex-analyst. Truly use his expertise. Include him in strategy sessions. If you expect him to be a glorified analyst relations person you will lose him quickly.

I was hired away from Gartner by a software security vendor who I won't name (just look at my LinkedIn profile). It was a consumer software vendor, not a network security vendor, so I did not make the potentially career damaging move to a vendor I covered. In my two years there the executive team did not ask for my advice once. I would get calls from CEOs of other tech firms asking for advice on strategy every month, yet my own employer just wanted me out there evangelizing. When I left, the execs took me out for drinks. The chairman of the company came over and asked without a trace of irony: "So, now that you are leaving, what do you really think we should be doing?" I gave him an earful while the CEO stood by aghast.

The drop-by briefing

I covered the drop-by briefing in detail in another chapter. Only a few vendors in any space reach out to the analyst in such an informal way. Do it.

The sales call briefing

Every analyst has to take his turn accompanying the Gartner sales rep on sales calls. Gartner has a business challenge. The sales rep sells the value of all the great research and instant access to subject matter experts, and the end-user clients shell out big dollars for that access, which is sold as a subscription. When renewal time comes around the sales rep has to demonstrate how valuable the relationship is so the client does not decide to drop the subscription or pare down how many "seats" they pay for. One of the ways a sales person can demonstrate that value is to bring a big name analyst by for an hour-long brain dump.

Before you become a Gartner client, you may be able to take advantage of this no-cost opportunity to interact with the analyst. Tell your rep that if she brings in the analyst you will sign up. That will accelerate the process. If an analyst visit can close a deal, the rep will pull strings to make it happen.

Don't treat the analyst visit like a briefing or mini-SAS day. This is different. Bombard the analyst with questions. Put him in the position of demonstrating his value. This is the only time the analyst will ever be selling you something. Make him earn it. When the sales rep calls you the next day, tell her how impressed you were (you will be), that you saw the value, and when can she send over the paper work? Now the rep feels that the analyst closed the deal, so you added to the analyst's reputation. And the analyst feels responsible for bringing you on board. It's just another subtle step along the path of your MQ plan.

Use these guerrilla tactics sparingly. They can be

powerful tools if applied correctly at the right time. Now on to the most direct and critical step to accomplishing your Magic Quadrant goal: responding to the MQ questionnaire.

CHAPTER NINETEEN

Responding to the MQ Questionnaire

If you have convinced the analyst that you belong on the MQ, you will eventually be asked to fill out the MQ Questionnaire. You may have to request this several times. You do not want to miss out because of an oversight on the part of the analyst. There are usually some cut-off rules the analyst will apply to keep the number of vendors down to a manageable amount. But if you can convince him that you are doing interesting things and moving the industry forward, you should still be able to get on it.

When you get the Questionnaire, begin working on the response immediately. There will be financial questions that require input from the CFO/CEO especially if you are publicly traded. It must be okay to reveal numbers that are never broken out in public statements because I see it done all the time for various industry analyst reports. Of course, the analysts keep those numbers confidential and do not publish them or share them with a competitor.

Every questionnaire for each Magic Quadrant is different, but the techniques and advice provided here are equally applicable to all.

The Questionnaire is a spread sheet with about 50 lines. It is usually broken into two sections; one to measure ability to execute and one to measure completeness of vision.

Answer them all honestly. The analysts fact-check when they can and apply the sniff test to anything you provide.

I remember putting together the Managed Security Service Provider MQ. A key measurement we selected was number of devices under management. I was friends with the AR guy at the firm who claimed to be the largest. He had come over with an acquisition, a company at which I had been an early employee. During the first briefing he flat out said they had 1,500 devices under management. He soon left the vendor and at the next briefing the new AR person said they had 1,100 devices under management. Then I went to a SAS day at one of their competitors in Boston. Their new CTO had just left the first company. I asked him how many devices they had under management when he left. He said no more than 550! So you can see, never lie to an analyst. Some vendors fudge their financials, confusing bookings with revenue, or using the number they would be at if they had been selling at list price instead of the typical discounts. Sure, round up. Everyone does. But if you have a flat year or a slight downturn, you could get in trouble since then you would be reporting a fall off in revenue for the year. At one point Gartner had a division, DataQuest, that was responsible for gathering market size data. When an analyst went to create an MQ he would get the numbers that DataQuest was using. I soon learned that that was useless. One of my least favorite vendors (remember the 70 page Power Point briefing from hell?) was reporting revenue figures for IDS that exceeded that of Cisco and yet I had never heard of their IDS product and they did not have a web page for it.

You will also need to reach out to product engineering to answer the feeds and speeds questions. Make sure that reported numbers jibe with the published numbers in your data sheets as well as any independent test results that an analyst will have access to. Don't forget that your competitors are spreading test result numbers that you have never seen and that, of course, demonstrate that the competitor's product is the best.

Be verbose in your answer. Give the short answer that the analyst can apply weighting factors to, but also explain any extenuating circumstances that show your product in the best light. This may be the first time you get to explain the secret sauce of your product in a way the analyst will focus on.

Gather all the data from finance and engineering, fill the spreadsheet out and get it back on time. No rush since the analyst is not waiting anxiously to start poring through the data you provide. The due date is fine. You can even beg for an extension. If you were on the previous MQ they really can't drop you for being late. But why give a bad impression when you are being evaluated?

By now you should be very familiar with the analyst's thinking. You questioned her on it during the briefings and SAS day. But you can still schedule an inquiry to ask clarification questions. This is the one time I would back off on the continual touch points. Just turn it around and get it back to her.

Schedule a last meeting with the entire team to get buy-in on what you are submitting. These are the numbers and answers that you are going to live with for at least six months.

Next, you will get a draft of what the analyst is going to say about you and the first look at the MQ graph. Schedule an inquiry immediately if you are well below where you expected. Analysts make mistakes. No irate call means they are on target, maybe they even put you too high and can safely lower your dot in the last balancing/moving that occurs before publishing. If you see a major mistake, let the analyst know. Some vendors are extremely good at bamboozling the analyst. There may be a vendor that everyone knows is going down the tubes. The CEO is a philanderer. The top sales guy was just hired away and took his entire team with him. The distributors are returning stock. They are under investigation for selling products to Iran. This is the time to let the analyst know. Don't engage in anything that could be considered tortious interference. Just suggest some things the analyst should look into. No innuendo, real extenuating circumstances. Odds are that your dot will be about where you expect it. Object to the surprises, ask the analyst where he would like to see improvement next year, and move on.

If you have crafted a plan and executed on it according to the guidance in this book, everything will go smoothly. Don't be like most vendors who scramble every year to respond. Avoid the fire drill.

CHAPTER TWENTY
What Not To Do

In a race UP and to the RIGHT there will always be losers. By now you can guess my advice if after all this work, you are ranked lower than you expected in the Magic Quadrant; stay the course. Keep on plugging away. Of course every organization has to choose what battles to fight. I highly suggest that taking Gartner to task publicly is a losing proposition. Let's look at two examples still talked about in analyst circles. First from a giant, Oracle, second from a small player, ZL Technologies.

Betsy Burton, one of Gartner's most senior analysts, once famously criticized Ellison in a report titled "Oracle Under Fire." She said prices were too high and data base performance was low and buggy. Ellison lashed back.

In a book about Oracle (Softwar: An intimate Portrait of Larry Ellison and Oracle, 2003) written primarily by Matthew Symonds, Larry Ellison says:

"Betsty Burton uses a more random approach: she publishes her results without any supporting data or details about her methodology. You can't check a damn thing. You have to take her word for it."

Ellison also went on the war path. He had his own people compile a list of all the times Gartner had been wrong in a crusade to discredit their insights. He tasked his team to go back through historical Gartner Research Notes and highlight all of Gartner's mistakes and mis-calls. Those documents have mysteriously disappeared but I recall they included the prediction that OS2 would become the operating system of choice for the enterprise and ATM-to-the-desktop would be the networking technology that would win over TCP/IP.

The goal of course was to taint Gartner's reputation and ability to predict winners and losers. Oracle was a Gartner client and spent big money on their relationship. Ellison had even appeared on the stage at Symposium. But he took criticism of his baby personally.

The results from Ellison's tirade are mixed. He generated a lot of attention and he surely alienated Betsy Burton. Oracle and Gartner are both doing very well today so obviously this clash of Titans did not result in the death of either.

My advise is that you should go to the mat with Gartner only if you are the billionaire CEO of a multi-billion dollar company.

In May, 2009 a small email archiving company, ZL Technologies (formally ZipLip), sued Gartner over the Magic Quadrant. According to Tom Foremski, writing at Silicon Valley Watcher their complaint included claims that:

- Gartner's use of their proprietary "Magic Quadrant" is misleading and favors large vendors with large sales and marketing budgets over smaller innovators such as ZL that have developed higher performing products.

- The complaint alleges: defamation; trade libel; false advertising; unfair competition; and negligent interference with prospective economic advantage.

- Fair Disclosure on Conflicts of Interest--Gartner generates its revenues from payments made by the same vendors whose products it evaluates. Similar to the new rules now being imposed on financial ratings agencies on Wall Street, Gartner should be required to disclose the revenues received from the vendors it ranks.

- Fair Disclosure on Evaluation Scores--The tech industry would benefit if Gartner were required to disclose more data in its evaluation process and disclose component scores so vendors know exactly where they are lacking and by how much and take corrective action. Currently, there is zero disclosure, which can lead to arbitrary placement, with no recourse and no basis for appeal.

This litany is practically the playbook for every vendor who has whined about their positioning in the Gartner Magic Quadrant. Is some of it true? Well, for sure large established vendors get preference. Don't forget that Gartner's client base is 80% late adaptors and the Magic Quadrants are targeted at their needs. Yes, analysts should be on top of their markets and they should be identifying disruptive changes. They do track the up and coming vendors and watch them carefully, but they are not going to push them UP and to the RIGHT prematurely. ZL used their suit to make a case that their email archiving product was faster than Symantec's product which Gartner had put in the Leaders Quadrant.

The judge in this case found predominantly in favor of Gartner. He gave ZL Technologies 30 days to respond to his judgement and then maintained his findings after ZL filed an update. ZL's statement about the judgement:

> "ZL believes that Gartner's overwhelming influence on large corporations' purchasing decisions, and its inaccurate ratings, including its bias in favor of large vendors, combine to pose major competitive hurdles that hurt smaller innovative vendors across all technology sectors. The harm falls not only on new and innovative

companies like ZL, but on the enterprise customers who receive faulty purchasing advice, and as a result overspend on inferior technology."

And two years later, after an expensive and fruitless battle, ZL Technologies proudly issued a press release when they were included as Visionaries in the Gartner Magic Quadrant.

"SAN JOSE, CA (December 15, 2011) -- ZL Technologies Inc., a leader in enterprise information archiving solutions for large enterprises, announced today it has earned a coveted spot in the "Visionaries" segment of Gartner's annual Magic Quadrant review of key vendors in the enterprise information archiving space."

"Coveted". Wow.

So, what do you do if you feel there has been an egregious miscarriage of justice? Work with Gartner to resolve it. Gartner *does* have an office of the ombudsman. Start there. Be professional. Do not make your grievance public. Keep it civil and do not attack the analyst personally.

CHAPTER TWENTY-ONE
Wrap up

The MQ plan is never complete. It is part of the process for any vendor in the technology space. The purpose and goal is to make sure that your position on the Magic Quadrant aligns with your true position in the market relative to the Gartner client base. Done properly, the MQ could be a true sign of a problem in your organization. You may not even see it coming. You think it is the economic conditions that led to flat sales for your products. But your competitors may be racing ahead because of a product feature they discovered that really addresses a customer problem. Maybe they have a better sales staff or their geographic location is better. Maybe they are not constrained by a scarcity of talented people to hire. Maybe their new CEO is an industry expert herself while your new CEO came from Procter and Gamble or GE and is trying to execute on a failing strategy. Maybe the market and the analysts picked up on this.

Treat the MQs seriously, just as the Gartner end-user clients do.

Did your new product revenue recently fall below your renewal level? That is a sure sign that you are coasting and about to fall. Your board may love it because your profitability is soaring and Wall Street is pushing your stock up. Maybe you are suffering from Christenson's innovator's dilemma. The technology shift is on and those upstart vendors that don't have to support legacy customers are getting all the new business.

This is why buyers need industry analysts. Analysts see these changes coming (if they are doing their job) and forewarn their clients.

According to Gideon Gartner, the founder of Gartner Group, the Magic Quadrant had its birth in a series of "stalking horses" he created. A stalking horse was meant to be a way for analysts to look at a particular space or trend in a new way. They would present these at internal meetings to generate discussion and insights that could inform Gartner's published reports. The stalking horses themselves were never meant to be published. At one such meeting Gideon suggested creating a chart with two axis to create a picture of a particular vendor-space. Thus, the Magic Quadrant was born, although never published as such while Gideon was at the helm.

From that simple beginning the Magic Quadrant has taken on a life of its own. There are hundreds of separate MQs, each devoted to a particular category, many apparently overlapping. To anyone outside the IT industry they present a confusing array of product options and a universe of diversity in product choice. The IT industry insiders that have to bring their products to market, especially to the enterprise, live and die by their position in the Magic Quadrant and examine the nuances presented in each report as it is published.

As I researched this book I encountered vehement reactions to the Magic Quadrant. They are viewed as arbitrary and tilted in favor of those vendors that spend the most with Gartner. But I also discovered that Gartner has invested much in improving the objectivity of their process. They have beefed up the Office of the Ombudsman to give vendors a channel to voice their protests.

Yes, you have to spend money to improve your recognition in any market. As I have stressed throughout this book there are strategic and tactical ways to invest your resources to ensure that you are accurately represented in the Magic Quadrant. Follow the MQ Plan you have created and you will see results in your journey UP and to the RIGHT.

APPENDIX I

Additional Resources

There are a few resources you can look to for additional information on the analyst industry as well as recommended reading.

Influencing the Influencers is a guide to analyst relations written by William S. Hopkins, the founder of the Knowledge Capital Group. Bill has been a Gartner analyst and has held marketing roles at several IT companies. The Knowledge Capital Group provides AR services including training and certification. I highly recommend Bill's book and engaging KCG to help build your AR team and processes.

Crossing the Chasm: Marketing and Selling High-Tech Products to Mainstream Customers by Geoffrey A. Moore (Aug 20, 2002) Many of Moore's concepts have entered the lexicon of technology business advancement. "Chasm," "bowling alley," even the progression from "early adaptors" to "late adaptors" are concepts that Moore originated. *Chasm* is required reading for anyone who wants to understand the path from startup to market leader.

Influence: Science and Practice by Robert B. Cialdini. Read this book for an understanding of the psychology of influence. It will give you great ideas of your own on how to instill an "inception point" in the analyst's mind.

Influencer Marketing: Who Really Influences Your Customers? by Duncan Brown and Nick Hayes. This book takes a much broader look at influencers and is applicable to consumer product companies as well as technology vendors who sell to large enterprises. A great read.

If you want to read a telling example of vendor frustration check out the complaint filed against Gartner by ZL Technologies.

Gartner's "Magic Quadrant" Goes To Court--ZL Technologies Lawsuit http://www.siliconvalleywatcher.com/mt/archives/2009/10/gartners_magic.php

To find independent analysts that cover your space use this directory curated by Barbara French: http://analystdirectory.barbarafrench.net/ Barbara was the managing director for the now-defunct Tekrati. She maintains the directory in her spare time. Today she is a Senior Director of analyst relations for a large network equipment vendor.

What the Plus! Google+ for the Rest of Us by Guy Kawasaki is a how-to guide that will help you delve into Google+.

The Innovator's Dilemma: The Revolutionary Book That Will Change the Way You Do Business by Clayton M. Christensen provides great insights into why established companies fail. It is based on the observation that industries are disrupted by newcomers that are not saddled with legacy technology and customers.

And finally, the author engages with many clients to assist in formulating their analyst strategy and MQ Plan. Visit www.AnalystInfluence.com to sign up for a monthly newsletter and a link to an original video lecture. Worksheets for creating your MQ Strategy and MQ Plan can be found there. You can also be put on the waiting list for the next **UP and to the RIGHT** two day seminar coming to a city near you.

APPENDIX II
GARTNER MQ FAQ

The following FAQ is provided by Gartner on their website. It was downloaded May 17, 2012.

Magic Quadrant and MarketScope: Frequently Asked Questions

Gartner follows a formal process to create Magic Quadrants and MarketScopes to ensure consistency in our ratings and placements. The questions that follow address what we hear most often from end-users and vendors about these processes.

Research Processes for Magic Quadrants and MarketScopes

What is the internal approval process for a new Magic Quadrant or MarketScope?

If an analyst wants to create a new Magic Quadrant or MarketScope, he or she proposes the research as part of a specific research agenda.

The proposal includes:
- The market definition
- Draft inclusion criteria
- Draft evaluation criteria

• Proposed model (Magic Quadrant or MarketScope) • Project team and time involved

The proposal goes through several internal levels of review, ending with the Senior Research Board, to ensure that we look across research agendas when we define a new market. Once approved, the new Magic Quadrant or MarketScope is added to the list of planned research on gartner.com. Magic Quadrants and MarketScopes are reviewed annually, and the title of the Magic Quadrant or MarketScope, along with the refresh date, is noted on the planned research list on gartner.com.

What is the process for an annual update to a previously published Magic Quadrant or MarketScope?

To ensure a current reflection of market conditions, an analyst proposes updating the Magic Quadrant or MarketScope as part of the agenda planning for the upcoming year for a specific research area. The update will include changes from the previous year to refine the market definition, vendor inclusion criteria and evaluation criteria, if required. The proposal must be accepted by the agenda manager and the analyst's team manager. No other approvals are needed. No change is needed to the list on gartner.com, unless the update falls beyond the one-year anniversary of the document.

How do you consolidate two or more previously

published Magic Quadrants or MarketScopes?

Analysts who want to consolidate two or more Magic Quadrants or MarketScopes are asked to retire the existing research documents and create a proposal for a new one. The proposal process is roughly the same as that explained above. The new market definition explains why the markets have been consolidated. The Magic Quadrants or MarketScopes to be replaced are retired (archived) 12 months from the published date. The list of planned research on gartner.com will show "retired" for the previously published documents. The consolidated MQ or MS is considered new research and listed as "upcoming" research on gartner.com.

What is the process for retiring a previously published Magic Quadrant and MarketScope?

Why would that happen?

Retirement of Magic Quadrants and MarketScopes follow a specific process. The analyst and relevant agenda manager evaluate whether a Magic Quadrant or MarketScope should be retired, based on decreased client interest in the overall market area or if certain changes to the market have occurred. If a particular Magic Quadrant or MarketScope is a low priority in terms of overall topic coverage or client demand for that research has declined, the decision may be to not update the Magic Quadrant or MarketScope. If the decision is made to retire the research, the "Refresh Date" field on gartner.com will say "retired," and the document will be archived a year after its publication date. The lead author will notify all vendors that participated in the now-retired Magic Quadrant or MarketScope that it will no longer be published.

Why doesn't Gartner share specific rating results of vendors?

Magic Quadrant or MarketScope authors collaborate to evaluate and score each vendor using a set of weighted criteria that are described within each methodology. The resulting scores are used to generate a Magic Quadrant position or MarketScope rating. Gartner does not provide specific scores because scores are based on not just quantitative elements, but qualitative as well. So it is not strictly a mathematical calculation. A vendor might earn a relatively high score in Product/Service because the quality, uniqueness and integration of its product/service elements is higher than other vendors', even if it lacks some of the features of other vendors. One area to look for where vendors scored particularly high is in its Strengths section; where it scored low is often reflected in the Cautions bullets. Again, this is not always the case, but it often is.

When and how are vendors contacted directly about a Magic Quadrant or MarketScope?

An analyst sends vendors an email letting them know of the creation of a new Magic Quadrant or MarketScope and requesting the appropriate contact to work with through the research process. (If the analyst already knows the contact at a vendor, this step may not be necessary.) Once the contact is confirmed, the analyst sends an email that explains the market definition, inclusion criteria, evaluation criteria and weights, research process and timeline. For a new Magic Quadrant or MarketScope, this initial vendor notification usually occurs between 8 and 16 weeks before the planned publication date. This time frame varies based on project complexity. The timing may be shorter for MQs/MSs that have been published more than once.

Are vendors contacted if they are dropped from a Magic Quadrant or MarketScope when it is updated?

Yes, vendors are notified in advance of publication that they will not be represented in the updated research, along with an explanation of why they will not be included. The published document will note that the vendor has been dropped and include a brief explanation of why that vendor no longer meets the inclusion criteria.

Can a vendor "opt in" or "opt out" of a Magic Quadrant or MarketScope?

No. Vendors are included in the research only if they meet the market definition and inclusion criteria established by the analyst. If a vendor meets the inclusion criteria, our process requires that it be represented in the Magic Quadrant or MarketScope. If a vendor does not meet the criteria, they will not be included as a participating vendor in the Magic Quadrant or MarketScope.

Are analysts required to ask vendors for information when creating a Magic Quadrant or MarketScope project?

Analysts are not required to solicit information from vendors when creating a Magic Quadrant or MarketScope. The analyst determines whether he or she has sufficient information through regular contact with vendors and customers in that market to develop the document without this input. Analysts may request information from vendors in the form of a questionnaire or a request for a briefing; often, the content from these requests is used for other research deliverables in addition to the Magic Quadrant or MarketScope.

Are analysts limited in the number of questions they can ask in their surveys?

No. Analysts are not restricted in the number of questions they can ask in their surveys, but there is suggested guidance that they keep the questions to a minimum and only ask for details that will help to fill in the gaps. Generally, if an analyst asks many questions in a survey, the chances are that he or she will be using response data in more deliverables than just a Magic Quadrant or MarketScope.

If the analyst does not require specific input from vendors, when are vendors notified that they will be represented in a Magic Quadrant or MarketScope report?

Vendors that meet the inclusion criteria and market definition are notified at the beginning of a Magic Quadrant or MarketScope project. Analysts send all included vendors an email notifying them of their inclusion. The email includes the market definition, inclusion criteria, evaluation criteria, weightings for each criteria and expected publish date of the research. Vendors are also sent a copy of the draft content and asked to check it to ensure accuracy prior to publication; they are given five business days for this factual review. The review is not an opportunity for the vendor to disagree about placement within a quadrant. Vendor responses back to the analyst need to be in writing. Analysts are encouraged to notify vendors once they have a sense of the approximate date that the draft will be sent for factual review.

What happens if a vendor declines to provide information requested by the analyst?

Analysts work with the information available to them from other sources, including publicly available information, feedback from our client base and industry contacts. The draft Magic Quadrant graphic or MarketScope table, along with specific content related to that vendor, is sent for factual review, following the standard process. A disclaimer is also added to the document:

<Vendor X> did not respond to requests for supplemental information or to review the draft contents of this document. The Gartner analysis is therefore based on other credible sources, including <insert any sources that apply, such as the following:>
- Public information
- <Y> discussions with users of this product

What assurances do vendors have that vendor-supplied references will be contacted?

If an analyst asks for and receives vendor-supplied references, he/she is required to contact those references and notify the vendor if he/she is unable to reach any of them.

What opportunity do vendors have to review the Magic Quadrant or MarketScope before it is published?

Vendors are given five business days to review relevant draft content, including the complete graphic (for example, with all named "dots" in the Magic Quadrant or the entire MarketScope table) and vendor-specific commentary for factual accuracy.

Is the data collection and review process the same for all vendors, even if they are not Gartner clients?

Yes, it is exactly the same. Client status has no bearing on our research processes.

What if a participating vendor disagrees with its position or the analyst's comments?

The first point of escalation is the analyst who created the research being questioned. Vendors should approach analysts with issues regarding facts, processes, methodologies or opinions expressed in research. The second point of escalation is the analyst's manager, whose role is to verify that all required methodologies and processes were followed by the analyst(s) and that all Research positions have been appropriately supported. The third is the Office of the Ombudsman.

Is there any attempt to coordinate the timing for Magic Quadrants and MarketScopes in related topic areas?

No, due to the breadth of coverage of the various topic areas it is not possible to coordinate the related topics between the number of analysts who cover these areas and their other commitments. However, information gathered during the preparation of a Magic Quadrant or MarketScope is often shared across related topic areas.

Where can I find more information about the Magic Quadrant and MarketScope and other Gartner methodologies on gartner.com?

For more details about Gartner Methodologies, go to the Methodologies page.

What do I do if want to excerpt this research or

buy reprints of it?

To excerpt research, email quote.requests@gartner.com, call +1 203 316 6178 or access the Quote Request details on g.com. To purchase reprints, contact reprints@gartner.com.

1318277R00099

Made in the USA
San Bernardino, CA
10 December 2012